THE bad habits OF JESUS

SHOWING US THE WAY TO LIVE RIGHT
IN A WORLD GONE WRONG

LEONARD SWEET

Tyndale House Publishers, Inc.
Carol Stream, Illinois

Library of Congress Cataloging-in-Publication Data

Names: Sweet, Leonard I., author.
Title: The bad habits of Jesus : showing us the way to live right in a world gone wrong / Leonard Sweet.
Description: Carol Stream, IL : Tyndale House Publishers, Inc., 2016. | Includes bibliographical references.
Identifiers: LCCN 2016028818 | ISBN 9781496417510 (sc)
Subjects: LCSH: Jesus Christ—Person and offices.
Classification: LCC BT203 .S94 2016 | DDC 232.9/03—dc23 LC record available at https://lccn.loc.gov/2016028818

Printed in the United States of America

22   21   20   19   18   17   16
 7   6   5   4   3   2   1

To Anne Mathews-Younes

A Living Lord's Prayer

whose spirit is the greatest legacy of E. Stanley Jones

CONTENTS

ACKNOWLEDGMENTS

WE LIVE IN A WORLD where *cool* has nothing to do with climate, *hip* is not a part of the body, and to say someone *killed it* doesn't mean they hurt anybody but brought something to life.

It has not been easy learning to speak and think in this new vernacular, where *bad* is good and where *cougar, trout,* and *salmon* have nothing to do with nature. I could not have made these transitions and translations without the help of my three youngest kids, Egil, Soren, and Thane. For their willingness to let their father sit on his kids' knees and learn from them, I am grateful. Even though this book was written in six weeks, when I didn't have time to have time, thanks to Elizabeth I always knew I needed to make time and learn how to take time to have time.

For the last two years I have served as Distinguished Visiting Professor at Tabor College. The Tabor master's students I taught in the spring of 2016 were some of the brightest and most innovative students with whom I have ever had the privilege of studying. I am jealous of Rick Bartlett and David Swisher for spending their full time with such stellar graduate students. For their insights on these "bad habits" during the course of this semester, I am grateful to Edith Buller-Breer, Greg Chewning, Aaron (Joseph) Duvall, Jon Esau, Vern Hyndman, Mary (Alexandra) Marintzer, Kurt McDonald, Kristen Poljansek, Aubrey Smith, Lee Waldron, and Joseph Wuest.

Books on the habits of Jesus have been plentiful (*The Jesus Habits*, *Habits of Grace*, *7 Habits of Jesus*, etc.). Since I had already done one book on how Jesus ate good food with bad people (*From Tablet to Table*), I gave Michael Waddell's idea of another "bad" book (i.e., bad habits) a standing observation when my agent, Mark Sweeney, gave it a standing ovation and kept clapping until I said yes to the project. Magriet Smit cheered me on daily while I was writing this over Christmas and reminded me that what loomed in front of me as one of the Alps could be an anthill if I approached it differently.

On January 28, 2016, I announced on my Facebook timeline that I was finishing up writing this book, and I invited people to submit their own nominations for the bad habits of Jesus. I then said that the ones I picked would be part of the book in some way, a new authorial device called *crowdsourcing*. So their entries on my timeline were also their permissions to use their quotes in the book. The response to my invitation was a flood. I have lifted out some of the ones that were the most provocative and the least covered in the book. Thanks to all my coauthors.

ACKNOWLEDGMENTS

Laughter does so much good for the body, mind, and spirit that you should call those who make you laugh your doctors. The doctor is always in when Landrum Leavell III is around. If you think Jesus turns his followers into sourpusses and crab apples, you need to meet Landrum. Lori Wagner is my right arm, left brain, and demolitions expert. She has edited everything I have written for the past seven years (as well as co-authored a novel with me) and was able to fit this bad-habits bombshell into her already-crowded schedule. When a metaphor misfires, that's on me. But there would be a lot more sputtering and lurching, and some loss-of-limb explosions in the political minefield that is language, without her roadside clearings and disarmings of my mindless metaphorical IEDs.

I finished this book while speaking twice a day in Kerala, India, at the Maramon Convention (2016), sponsored by the Mar Thoma Syrian Church. For me this annual camp-meeting, the largest gathering of Christians in Asia (150,000–200,000), was a way of following in the footsteps of one of my missionary heroes, E. Stanley Jones. I have already dedicated a book to him. I now dedicate this book to my traveling companion in India, Anne Mathews-Younes, the granddaughter of E. Stanley Jones. In two weeks of traveling together I could not find even a sliver of a bad habit, much less a single one. I hope, now that I've dedicated this book to her, she won't reveal my multitude of badnesses.

Leonard Sweet
ORCAS ISLAND
PENTECOST SUNDAY, 2016

A TROUBLING HOPE
FOR A TROUBLED WORLD

INTRODUCTION

Jesus is God's way of getting rid of a bad reputation.
JOHN KILLINGER

EVEN THOUGH JESUS was God's Son, he had habits and behaviors that were considered bad in the eyes of the culture of his day. Some of them seem wrong even today. All of Jesus' "bad habits," however, reveal truths about God's love and message that are vital for us.

Some of these bad habits were seen as sins against the Torah. Some were bad habits of hygiene and holiness. In this book, we will explore the words and actions of Jesus, those that his religious culture considered offensive, and reframe them for a twenty-first-century world using fresh metaphors and contemporary language.

Would Jesus offend you today? If not, you are missing the scandalous nature of Jesus the rabble-rousing rabbi as told in the stories of the Gospels. Jesus revealed a God who has gone to great trouble over every person in every corner of the world. No one is not worth God's trouble. That is why Jesus came to trouble us with the truth: that it is only in being "bad" in the eyes of the world that we can be "good" in the eyes of God.

Teresa of Ávila once heard Christ say to her in prayer, "See yourself in me." When we find ourselves in Christ, we start to find Christ in ourselves and in each other. Life falls into place when Jesus gets first place. Life is what you make it. Abundant life is what Jesus makes it. Only a right relationship with Christ will right the world.

And a good way to get that relationship started and keep it going is to make his habits our own. Even his bad habits. *Especially* his bad habits.

JESUS SPIT

CHAPTER ONE

IN THE ORIGINAL FILM VERSION of *Charlie and the Chocolate Factory*, Willy Wonka gives Mrs. Teevee a rainbow drop and encourages her to suck on it and then spit to see the rainbow of colors. Violet, who later would have to be rolled to the juicing room, tells Wonka, "Spitting's a dirty habit!"

She's right, of course. Just ask your mother. Or ask the Chinese, whose bureaucrats have been on a sustained campaign against public spitting. Spitting in public has been against the law in numerous US states and is still on the books in five of them.

In Jesus' day, spitting was equally obnoxious. It was a

gross insult to spit at someone, in someone's presence, or especially in someone's face. It was rude to spit on the ground in front of a person. We see the impact and insult of spitting in Jesus' humiliation by the guards,[1] and in the Hebrew Scriptures as well.[2]

> *I did not hide my face from mocking and spitting.*
>
> ISAIAH 50:6

As strange as it may seem, Jesus spit. Jesus used spit on three different occasions in conjunction with a healing. The most unusual usage was when he used spit to make mud and applied it to a blind man's eyes, giving new meaning to the phrase "as clear as mud." While his followers busied themselves with the theology behind the man's suffering, Jesus busied himself giving the blind sight.[3]

Imagine the shock—or perhaps not—when Jesus faced the man and spat upon the ground. Perhaps everyone around him was nodding in approval, thinking that Jesus was obviously showing his contempt for the outcast Jew. But then Jesus did the unthinkable. He reached down, gathered up the spittle and some dirt, made a poultice of mud, and then applied the clay to the man's eyes.

From a gesture of insult, Jesus created a magnificent and powerful blessing. And isn't that how God works anyway?

The origin of Jesus' actions can be seen in Genesis 2,

when God creates humankind from earth and water, all origi-
nating from the mouth of God. God speaks in Genesis 1:26:
"Let us make humankind in our image" (NRSV).

> Now no shrub had yet appeared on the earth and no
> plant had yet sprung up, for the LORD God had not
> sent rain on the earth and there was no one to work
> the ground, but streams came up from the earth
> and watered the whole surface of the ground. Then
> the LORD God formed a man from the dust of the
> ground and breathed into his nostrils the breath of
> life, and the man became a living being.[4]

Jesus' healings spit in the eye of tradition and illuminate
the truth of God's love even for the outcasts. Jesus' spit is
also a sign of his messianic
identity and his relationship to the Grand Potter,
the Creator of all things,
the Giver of life, and the
Restorer of the human condition. Jesus does not lord it
over others from above but
stays close to the earth in his
stories, in his language, in
his imagination, and in his reasoning.

MORE BAD HABITS

**Spitting on people (tongue
and eyes with mud)—I bet
he healed ears with wet
willies!**

ALLEN GRIFFIN

Jesus' bad habit is a reminder to us that sometimes in
order to incarnate Jesus within a blind and confusing world,

it means we need to touch some dirt and spit in order to channel Christ's healing and wholeness. You can't up-up-and-away in creativity and innovation without spending down-on-the-ground time in the muck and mire.

Jesus' bad spitting habit is a reminder for us to take off our coats, spit on our hands, and get down and dirty in ministry and mission. For Jesus, dirtiness more than cleanliness is next to godliness. You might even call the twelve disciples the original Dirty Dozen. They were constantly being cajoled by Jesus to get their hands dirty in the grime and slime of the world's misery and pain and to approach everyone they met as people moving toward a future that transcended their present—"it does not yet appear what we shall be."[5] There is something *so* Jesus about the first Baptist church on English soil being founded at "Spitalfields" (in 1612).

For Jesus, clean hands reveal a dirty heart; dirty hands reveal a clean heart. In fact, our entry through the Pearly Gates may hinge on this question: "Let me see your hands. Have you gotten your hands dirty for the sake of the gospel?"

Truth came into the world—not abstract, pure, and antiseptic, but cradled in dirt, water, and mud, and mangered in

> **MORE BAD HABITS** 💬
>
> **When my mom would sweep the wood floors, she would always say, "Don't walk through my dirt!" Jesus is always walking through my dirt! (Dirty roads, dirty people.)**
>
> **BARRY D. CRAM**

mystery. The First Testament begins with a story about dirt and the first Adam: "God formed Man out of dirt from the ground." The Second Testament begins with a story about dirt and the second Adam: "The Word became dirt."[6]

Few stories are more deserving of documentaries and a movie than the story of Mama Heidi.[7] After missionary Heidi Baker and her husband earned their PhDs, God told Heidi, "Sit in the dust." She had no idea what that meant, but she prayed to be led. And God led her to a dump in Mozambique where she did what she was told and sat in the dust and dirt and there discovered her mission. Eventually she became a leading force in Mozambique for getting some seven thousand orphans adopted and ordaining six thousand pastors in the bush.

The gate to God swings open in every speck of dust. There are flowers in every dustbin, and dustups and dustheaps can be depositories of the divine.

An incredible movement of God began when Heidi Baker got down and dirty with God. How far down was God willing to go to lift us up? The filthiest parts of the human body in the first century were your feet. You could not even require slaves to wash their master's feet. Yet Jesus showed how far down God was willing to go to reach us by getting on his hands and knees and washing his disciples' feet. You don't wash anyone's feet without getting your hands dirty and wet.

When we get down and dirty, we hit pay dirt. Until we get our hands dirty and wet, until we can endure the spit, the grime, the mud, and the sludge of humanity's poor, sick, and dying, we can't be the "Potter's hands" of renewal and restoration for a dry and dusty world.

For Jesus the glamour is always in the grime. Jesus turns humus into humans, dirt into miracles, mud galoshes into miracles galore. The spittle of Jesus is the water of life to a hurting world. Only Jesus can create wholeness and restore us to the human beings we were meant to be. As the church we can be Jesus to the world, but only if we are not afraid of the spit and the dirt. To lose our earthiness is to lose our humility, which, in the end, is to lose our humanity.

God made the first Adam out of dirt and water. God brought the second Adam into the world upon a dirt floor amid the drool of animals. And God continues to manifest God's presence, power, and healing wherever Jesus is to be found through his human bride, the church.

Even today, God still turns dirt into grass, dirt into glass, dirt into diamonds, dirt into divinity. Because of Jesus, the last Adam, wherever sin and loss is present, God has the power to remake us and restore us out of "Godspit," God's own flesh and blood rebreathed by life-giving Spirit.[8] In a sense, this is our baptism—from the waters of the depths of the womb, we emerge filled with the "living waters" of God within us.

And no one is ever too far gone to be remade, reformed, revisioned, restored by the heavenly Potter. Without the breath (and spittle) of God, we are mere broken and lifeless clay. But when the waters of the Holy Spirit flow upon us, we can be anything God wants us to be.

When our hymn writers wanted to convey that we're all

All go to one place. All are from the dust,
and to dust all return.

ECCLESIASTES 3:20, ESV

dirt, they used spitfire metaphors like "wretch" and "worm."[9] As bad to our self-esteem as "wretch" and "worm" may be, the prophet Isaiah said that our righteousness is even worse: it is no better than soiled linen.[10] That said, you don't run away from the dirty laundry but face it. When Mary rushed toward a pile of soiled linen in the tomb, she bumped into an angel.

The gospel keeps your heart humble (heart in the kitchen), your head confident (head in the sky), and your hands courageous (hands in the dirt). As Paul says, "I can do all things [you can't get more confident than that] through Christ [you can't get more humble than that] who gives me courage."[11]

The world is afraid of touch, afraid of dirt, afraid of spit (at least spit that leaves the boundary of the body), afraid of seeing what we do not want to see. And yet there is usually no reproduction without the sharing of spit that we call kissing. It's like that, too, with Jesus. It's easy to love Jesus when it's tidy, hip, and clean. It's easier to donate money than to put our hand in the hand of a man or a woman who looks dirty, down, and drowned with mud. Yet the church of Jesus is not meant to be a hideaway but a hostel for all of God's dirtiest who need restoration and healing.

Just because we are "earthen vessels" doesn't mean we

need pampering, but we do need damping and molding. The God who created the heavens and the earth lived in an earthen vessel, a body, for thirty-three years. Jesus witnessed to the world God's blessing of the human body as the dwelling place of the fullness and holiness of God.

The Pharisees looked everywhere to things that pointed to the divine. Jesus looked everywhere to things that presenced the divine. When nature sings God's praise and signs God's glory,[12] it is not God singing and God signing. God is singing through creation; creation is not singing as God. Now, many of us are like Jacob and sleep through the presence of God. When Jacob awoke from his dream, he thought, "Surely the LORD is in this place, and I was not aware of it."[13] For Jesus, spirituality was something "down to earth." It was from the ground up, not from the sky down. The best translation of Psalm 16:8 is not "I have set the LORD always before me" but "I am ever mindful of the LORD's presence."[14]

> ### MORE BAD HABITS
>
> **Jesus insisted on washing his disciples' feet at suppertime but allowed some of them to skip out on hand washing before meals.**
>
> **BETTY J. JACKSON**

Proverbs 3:6 (RSV) reads, "In all your ways acknowledge [*da'ehu*, "know"] him." We give praise to God and deepen our relationship with God in everything we do, in every feature and function of human behavior, not just in explicitly holy acts. This is especially true in our relationships. When we draw near to each other (*qereb*), God approaches or draws near to us (*qarab*). Jesus says, "Where two or three gather in my name, there am I with them."[15]

To be a preacher—and we are all preachers—is to look every day for unexpected pulpits from which to preach. And for Jesus a lot of these unexpected pulpits were found in creation.

The first production in England of Friedrich Schiller's play *The Maid of Orleans*, a story about Joan of Arc, featured one of the greatest props ever conceived for the stage. While hugging close to Schiller's original play, the producers added one new prop, the only prop used in the whole production. Joan of Arc sees a helmet just brought in from the battlefield and exclaims, "It is mine!" This helmet is a clump of wet clay molded around Joan's head. It looks like a queen's headdress, but it dirties the hands of all who touch it, who then leave muddy streaks everywhere they go.

Such are the saints in God's Kingdom. A saint is both one who is pure and one who is tainted but who uses these "taints" to paint beauty, truth, and goodness—just as Jesus used his spit, his feet of clay, to make mud pies of healing for a maimed world.

To add bad habit upon bad habit, Jesus didn't put conditions on his healing. When Jesus saw blind Bartimaeus, he asked him "What can I do for you?" Bartimaeus answered, "Give me back my sight." Jesus gave him what he asked for. No questions asked; no conditions made. Jesus did not ask Bartimaeus to become his disciple, either to get the cure or to show gratitude for the cure. He was free to go his own way. Whereupon Bartimaeus followed Jesus.[16]

JESUS PROCRASTINATED

CHAPTER TWO

JESUS WAS A SERIAL PROCRASTINATOR, which meant he was often late.

Being late is as much a habit as being on time is. There are, however, degrees of tardiness and differing definitions of "on time." Consider the difference between walking into English class after the bell and arriving a couple of hours after a 911 call for help. One will get you detention, but the other has deadly consequences.

On at least two occasions, Jesus was late, and it cost someone her or his life. The first was Jairus's twelve-year-old daughter. Jesus stopped to help a sick woman while he was on his way to help the little girl. Before he got there, a message came that he was too late and that the grieving father shouldn't bother Jesus anymore. Jesus' subsequent actions demonstrate that God is not confined to linear timelines and time zones. God exists outside of time, and time has no meaning or value in eternity.[1] But God, the Eternal Now, is very concerned with how we steward our "nows" on this side of eternity.[2]

The second instance was his intentional tardiness when asked to come and heal one of his best friends, Lazarus. Upon arriving after the funeral, Jesus said that he had even shown up late purposefully. Mary and Martha's reactions are common among those who don't understand that God doesn't *tell* time, he *makes* it. Jesus shows his humanity at Lazarus's tomb by weeping, and then shows his divinity by speaking—"Come forth." Jesus stops clocks and starts hearts.

Humans are reactive to time; God is proactive with time. We operate within it; God operates outside of it. Jesus accomplished his mission in his time, not theirs or ours.

Our understanding of God's time zone is imperative to following Jesus. In each case of procrastination, ultimately Jesus was able to display his power over each individual's most serious point in time—death. We frantically pace, wearing out the waiting-room carpets of physicians and therapists because we don't trust God's timing.

In 1994, former New Jersey Governor Tom Kean (who later chaired the 9-11 Commission) invited me to Drew University to be dean and vice president of academic affairs under his presidency. I received the equivalent of an advanced degree in governance and administration under his tutelage and was amazed at the range of his stories. Maybe my favorite Kean story is of fellow New Jerseyan William F. Allen, who in 1883 "pulled off a miracle." What he did was to get not just an entire coast to pull in sync, but an entire nation. In Kean's words,

> Until high noon on October 18, 1883, every rail line ran on its own time. Every train station set its own clocks by the sun. So when it was noon in New York, it was 11:58 in Trenton and 11:56 in Camden, and so on. Pure chaos. Allen was chosen to sort out this mess, and after eight years he convinced the nation to adopt the time zones that we have today.

The task the church faces is a lot like Allen's, except we are trying to get people to adopt the time zone of eternity. As my mother, Mabel Boggs Sweet, used to put it, "God's clock keeps perfect time."

Jesus didn't procrastinate due to slackness or indecision or perfectionism or fear of moving forward. Jesus delayed doing what he wanted or needed to do because the timing wasn't right, because he was telling time by his Father's clock and making the most of the time his Father had given him.

Jesus stalled because "there is a proper time and procedure for every matter."[3] High procrastination for Jesus was less about putting off doing things than about waiting for the right moment to do things, which often conflicted with the timetables and schedules of everyone else.

Disciples of Jesus with this bad habit will be hard to predict because we are constantly being created anew and sent to do things we had no intention of doing or going places we had no intention of going or meeting people we had no intention of meeting.

Jesus is the most creative person who ever lived. His life, death, and resurrection are the very definitions of creativity. The most creative acts in history are God-generated acts. It shouldn't surprise us that creative people are often chronic procrastinators. Creatives generate more ideas than they can pursue, which is one reason they are not the risk takers they are often made out to be. They tend to be cautious about the ideas on which they expend their energy.

Hence some forms of procrastination are good strategies for moving forward. But Jesus also made clear that some forms of delay are never good:

- Never delay healing a broken relationship.[4]
- Don't let the sun go down on your wrath.[5]
- Go quickly to do what God is calling you to do.[6]

It is not the "decay of delay" but the pray and play of delay that incubates creativity and ensures its success. Procrastination provides a delay that gives space for all sorts of accomplishments.

Alfred Brendel (b. 1931) is an Austrian musician and poet who some have claimed is one of the greatest pianists of all time. One Beethoven sonata may contain 30,000 to 50,000 notes, and Brendel memorized Beethoven's entire corpus of sonatas. That's more than a million notes memorized. In his collection of essays and lectures titled *Music, Sense and Nonsense*, Brendel makes the case for a threefold responsibility of any creative performer to the original creativity of the artist: "as curator of a museum, as executor of a will, and as obstetrician."[7] Procrastination is involved in all three capacities.

MORE BAD HABITS

He kept an imbalanced and immoderate schedule. The Master Planner was a disaster at planning.

LEN CALHOUN

First, procrastination involves making sure one is in relationship with the composer and can curate the memory through prayer and meditation. Jesus was always connecting with his Father and making sure he was about his Father's business and conserving the heirlooms of his birthright. Sometimes delay is the best strategy for dealing with a problem, especially problems that have not been prayed over enough in the heart or played about enough in the mind. "Suppose one of you wants to build a tower. Won't you first sit down and estimate the cost to see if you have enough money to complete it? For if you lay the foundation and are not able to finish it, everyone who sees it will ridicule you."[8]

Second, procrastination enables familiarity with the estate and the last will and testament so that one can accurately follow the intentions of the Creator. Jesus seems to have memorized the Hebrew Scriptures and was continually seeing all of life through the lens of the First Testament. But every executor must exercise his or her own judgment and use intuition in the awakening of new zeal. The implementation of intuition trumps the implementation of intention. Intuition is knowing beyond logic, knowing the voice beyond the voice of the ancestors or the authorities. Postponing is not always a malfunctioning or a stalling but sometimes is a reckoning or honing of the idea and a reconnoitering with critics to see if it can withstand scrutiny. I have had some "brilliant" strokes of genius that others quickly perceived were so profoundly ill conceived, with reasoning so feeble, evidence so thin, and the conclusion such a glaring non sequitur, that procrastination saved me from huge embarrassment and error.

Third, procrastination involves the birth of something new and fresh. The connection between birth and creativity is a long-standing one, but one that has sometimes led even the best and brightest in the wrong directions. As recently as 1956, Freud's disciple and biographer Ernest Jones told a New York audience that creative thinking was male compensation for the inability to give birth. My mother used to argue that because women were more creative biologically than men, they were also more creative intellectually than men. Suffice it to say that whether male or female, we are all in the birthing business, and the greatest birth story we will ever be a part of is the birth of Jesus in each one of us.

As anyone who has ever given birth will testify, births don't often happen when they're scheduled or when they're predicted. Births take place when there is a readiness for arrival, when the time is right and the conditions are conducive for survival. Without this delay for the right moment of delivery, as Horace quipped, mountains of upheaval can bring forth only a meager mouse. This kind of procrastination commonly involves much suffering and anguish. With the cross in his sights, Jesus said, "I am in anguish until it be accomplished."[9] Jesus' death throes are birth pangs of new life. Birthing new life has always involved the risk of death, and the new birth of Christ in every one of us entails the death of self. The cross is not a giant plus symbol. It is an *I* crossed out.

> **MORE BAD HABITS** 💬
>
> **[He] put people above personal schedule and ideology.**
>
> **MATT BEAKES**

We add a candle every birthday. Jesus' birthday never adds candles. Jesus is the Eternal Contemporary, Emmanuel, God-with-us for every generation. When he is born in us, we become his candles that go into the world and light not a cake but the darkness. Jesus preached—but he is not a preacher; Jesus taught—but he is not a teacher; Jesus healed—but he is not a healer. Jesus is Lord and Savior, King of kings and Lord of lords, Emmanuel.

The church is so busy about so many things. We would be well advised to learn Jesus' bad habit of procrastination. We especially need to learn to wait on Jesus, which has both a Martha and a Mary meaning. There is the "waiter" meaning of "waiting on Jesus," which means serving him by serving others. To put the interests of others before our own is not to be weak but to be strong enough to transcend selfishness. That's why love is only for the strong, not the weak. Only the strong can love. Even when Jesus was being whipped and driven to his crucifixion, his thoughts were not about himself but about others . . . and us. "Daughters of Jerusalem, don't cry for me; cry for yourselves and your children."[10]

Then there is the "await" meaning of "waiting on Jesus," which means patiently waiting without hating or wearing out the carpets with our pacing and fretting, sitting at his feet upon his arrival, leaning into his presence, and learning to put on the mind of Christ. I used to hear "Cast all your cares on him because he cares for you"[11] as "Cast all your cares on him because he cares for your work, your diligence, your mission." But the actual passage says that God cares for *you*.

If we procrastinated as Jesus did, we might discover that God cares for the servant more than the servant's service.

JESUS APPEARED
WASTEFUL

CHAPTER THREE

MY MOTHER LIKED TO SERVE Cream of Wheat for breakfast. I hated this white mush in the mouth. One morning I uncharitably compared my mother's servings of instant Cream of Wheat to her mother's (my Appalachian Gramma's) grits and hominy she made from scratch on a wood-fired stove. Mother glared in response and scooped out a giant bowl of white, watery gruel and announced I wasn't getting up from the table until it was gone.

Her reasoning was not that one of her sons had pointed out her culinary failings as a daughter and mother. Instead, she lectured my brothers and me on wasting food and added that there were kids in India starving. "I don't think that even *they* would eat this," I sassed back. It was a long morning.

I have since then learned the importance of not wasting food, or time, or money, or words. But when I reached adulthood, I had to totally redefine what it meant to be wasteful. I had to define waste in Jesus' terms.

> **MORE BAD HABITS** 💬
>
> **Spending money on crazy gestures like MM with the perfume on his feet. #notverydaveramsey**
>
> **RACHAEL BARTOO ROBESON**

At first, it seemed that, like my mother, Jesus opposed waste. "Gather up the fragments left over, that nothing may be lost," he said of the bits of bread left over from his miracle on the mountainside.[1] Jesus certainly didn't waste time in his ministry, either. He walked relentlessly from town to town, preaching and teaching up until the day of his death. And he criticized those who would squander the money of the Master. Jesus didn't waste. Or did he?

On more than one occasion in the Scriptures, Jesus himself is accused of wastefulness, or accused of condoning wastefulness, lavishness.

He is accused of being a glutton and a drunkard: "The Son of Man came eating and drinking, and they say, 'Here is a glutton and a drunkard, a friend of tax collectors and sinners.'"[2]

Jesus was told by the Pharisees that he was wasting his time when he sat down to eat with "sinners." Even his disciples thought he was wasting his time and reputation when he spoke to the woman at the well or spent time with children.

When Jesus fed five thousand people who came to hear him on a hillside, there were twelve baskets of food left over, one doggie bag for each disciple.[3] What did the disciples do with Jesus' leftovers? We don't know for sure, but we can be sure they didn't waste them. Perhaps they used them to tell the story of a little boy who gave all he had.

Jesus' lavish demonstration of abundance resulted in overflowing baskets, enough to feed everyone there and many more. And he repeated the miracle among four thousand more, this time with seven baskets left over.[4] Each time, the food was much more than was needed. And Jesus didn't seem concerned about what became of the leftover baskets. His only thought was to demonstrate the majesty and the meaning of God's abundance.

The promise of the Story told in Scripture is a whole world swept up into the glory, grandeur, and goodness of God. God's promise to us is a land flowing with milk and honey, not misery and famine, poverty and disease. Creation is a place of abundance and bounty. When Jesus described the Kingdom of God to his disciples, he described a mustard seed that would multiply wildly and spread rampantly and lavishly through the land. He described yeast kneaded into bread until it had been worked all through the dough, which would rise uncontrollably into a rich, leavened bread. Jesus' descriptions are not of scarcity and asceticism but of abundance—bread that will expand to feed a world, a tree that will feed and house all within its branches.

Almost every time Jesus taught or spent time with people,

it was in the context of a meal.[5] We know that in some cases, banquets were held in his honor, as in the case of Levi (Matthew) the tax collector. And at no time does Jesus seem concerned about the amount of food abounding or about the wasted time preparing it.

In the story of Mary and Martha, Jesus condones Mary's "wasting" of time with him rather than toiling away in the kitchen with her anxious sister, Martha. And when he turns water into wine while attending a wedding in Cana, he makes so much of the sweet, rich, best-in-the-house drink that it's doubtful the guests could possibly consume it all in that last day of nuptial celebrations.

But food and drink wasn't the only way in which Jesus was "wasteful." Perhaps the most dramatic example of Jesus' wastefulness was when he allowed Mary to pour an expensive vial of perfume on his feet and rub it in with her hair. Judas was livid. All he saw was a year's salary poured down the drain. All he saw was spendthrift wastage, and he called Jesus on it.

Jesus' response is the essence of what he expects from his followers today—to surrender their all to him. To put at his disposal and that of the Kingdom all their possessions, all their time, all their abilities, even their very lives. The world will say, "What a waste!" but Jesus will say, "Well done."

Dionysius was a pagan scholar who converted to Christ and became bishop of Alexandria in 247 CE, a position he held until his death in 268. In a letter to fellow Christians, Dionysius describes a plague that struck Alexandria. Some suspect this plague took Dionysius's life. Here is what he says:

> Most of our brethren were unsparing in their
> exceeding love and brotherly kindness. They held
> fast to each other and visited the sick fearlessly,
> and ministered to them continually, serving them
> in Christ. And they died with them most joyfully,
> taking the affliction of others, and drawing the
> sickness from their neighbors to themselves and
> willingly receiving their pains. . . . But with the
> heathen everything was quite otherwise. They
> deserted those who began to be sick, and fled from
> their dearest friends. And they cast them out into the
> streets where they were half dead, and left the dead
> like refuse, unburied.[6]

One scholar who read Dionysius's words wrote, "When the life of the Christian group is recognizably different from the life of the world outside, then no tricks are needed to attract people."[7]

God has created life and all creation with plenitude, not scarcity. A scarcity mind-set is either-or thinking; a plenitude mind-set is both-and, and-also thinking. We share out of God's abundance, not scarcity. There is plenty to share in Jesus' Kingdom, an overflowing bounty at the messianic feast, more than enough at God's table.

For Jesus, maturity as a follower is not learning how to

save (Jesus has much to say about those who hoard rather than rejoicing in the moment) but learning how to spend abundantly in ways that sow God's love and grace into a hungry and thirsty world. A Jesus follower is not a waster of blessings, but a Jesus follower learns to waste wisely—to luxuriate and revel in the abundant blessings of God.

Jesus' hospitality boasts a dominant characteristic: it exceeds expectations. Jesus is always going overboard in hospitality. Jesus is a bad planner. He makes too much wine. He makes too much food. There are always leftovers, always seconds, when Jesus is the host.

There are two theological words for this: *supererogation*, which means doing above and beyond what is expected or even appropriate, and *nimiety*, which means the state of excess.

God created life and all creation with plenitude, not scarcity.[8] There is plenty to share. Jesus does not have an economics of scarcity, but an economics of abundance. To be a disciple of Jesus is to display hospitality as an act of supererogation, an exercise in nimiety. Jesus wants us to go the second mile, give the second coat, and maybe even give the second kidney.[9]

> *Nature is never spent;*
> *There lives the dearest freshness deep down things.*
> GERARD MANLEY HOPKINS

Life is what you make it. Abundant life is what Jesus makes it.

A wasted life is a life without Jesus in it. When Judas realized what he had done in betraying Jesus, he threw the silver pieces paid to him into the Temple sanctuary and then left and hanged himself. We could look at the wasted silver pieces, a wealth of money just thrown away. Or we could look at Judas and say, "What a wasted life!"

God's abundance is not about earthly wealth but about heavenly wealth. Like the lost sheep, the lost coin, or the lost son, whenever a soul is lost and then found, a time of great rejoicing bursts forth. Neighbors are called, a calf is prepared, a celebration breaks out. When one of God's lost comes home, rejoicing resounds in all the company of heaven. God's abundance is fully poured out, even for one. When even one lost is found, God gives a party! And it's always in the company of others, who know what a joy it is when a life is no longer wasted.

God's abundant love, grace, blessings, and promise are waiting for every one of us.

God's promise is all about abundance. When we pledge our lives to the Lord, God lavishes abundance upon us—abundant mercy, abundant fruitfulness, abundant feasting, abundant forgiveness. Abundant love.

This is the meaning of the parable of the "wasteful manager."[10] Resources are not wasted when they are building relationships or helping others or honoring the Son.

Mary's anointing of Jesus with expensive perfume was

enough to cause Judas to betray him. Judas believed that having money (by selling the perfume or by making a deal with the Pharisees) would make him happier than having Jesus. But Mary's "wastefulness" was not waste but worship. She knew that the perfume was costly. But she also knew that Jesus' gift to her and others was priceless.

Abundant love is never a waste of time. Worship is never a waste of time.

Jesus spent his time with many whom the Pharisees felt were wasted effort. But Jesus tells us in the parable of the sower that God sows the seeds of invitation upon all people. Some fall upon rocky ground, some fall among weeds, and some will grow to bear fruit. God's blessings are never wasted. God, who sees every sparrow fall, will pause to go after one sheep who has wandered away in error. And God will rejoice with all of the company of heaven, will lavish a banquet of abundance upon all, when that one sheep returns home again.

God's abundant grace knows no boundaries. After all, what could be more "wasteful" than Jesus laying down his life for all of us?

Our sense of wastefulness is like our sense of fairness, justice, and rightness. It is in direct opposition to God's sense of wastefulness. For God, the only wastefulness is a life without Jesus in it—a wasting of goodness, a wasting of beauty, a wasting of truth. God is about abundant mercy and extravagant love.

We, too, like Jesus, must cultivate the habit of being, in everything we do, wasteful in mercy, extraordinary in love, and extravagant in worship of Jesus the Christ.

Case Study: The Waste Story of the Wedding Feast in Cana of Galilee

It is every host's nightmare—running out of food and drink before running out of guests. What to do?

In the story of Jesus' debut miracle, a host finds himself in exactly that sticky situation. The gathering is nothing less than a wedding feast, one of the most socially significant and pub-

MORE BAD HABITS

He fed 4,000 people without them working for it.

GARY FRIEZE

licly important events any family could host. No matter how lavish twenty-first-century weddings have become—with average price tags inching their way to $40,000—our modern destination weddings have nothing on wedding celebrations held in the first century.

With "rapid transportation" being a donkey, it would take guests days, maybe up to a week, to reach the site of the wedding. Obviously guests did not turn around and start back after the ceremony and a meal. A wedding typically lasted for a week, and the wedding was more like the camp meetings of the past than the weddings of today. The bridegroom and his family were responsible for providing food and drink for all the guests during this extended period of celebration. Stockpiling the needed provisions was a serious responsibility. The family's reputation would stand or fall on their ability to offer genuine and generous hospitality to all who honored the bride and groom with their presence.

The wedding in Cana is such an affair. Although it is not specifically identified as a wedding of someone in Jesus' family, details suggest that this was a relative. Mary is already there when Jesus and his disciples, who "had also been invited,"[11] arrive—apparently well into the week of festivities. After the wedding, Jesus, his disciples, his mother, and his brothers (who were also in attendance) all travel together to Capernaum. Mary's eagle eye on the food and wine supplies suggests that she had a familial concern with everything going smoothly. Generally, invited guests don't show concern about a wine shortage; they just complain about it. It is family members who worry.

When Mary does notice that the wine supply has run out, she turns to her firstborn and announces, "They have no wine." Jesus' reply is surprisingly abrupt—"Woman, what concern is that to you and to me? My hour has not yet come." Literally Jesus' response is "What to me and to you?" It is not necessarily rude, but neither is this answer a soothing word to a fretful mother, especially as Jesus addresses Mary (as he does on the cross) by the generic *woman* and not by any familial title.

This response, even more than the water being turned into wine, might be identified as the first true sign that Jesus has now entered into his official public ministry, that he now fully embraces his messianic identity. No longer is he "Mary's son." No longer is he beholden to the kinship constraints of his earthly family. Jesus is now all about his Father's business. Jesus is starting on the path he has been born to walk.

Instead of being put off by Jesus' words, Mary responds not with feelings of hurt or assertions of her parental authority, but with a defiant expression of faith. Mary never tells Jesus what to do. Instead, she tells the servants at the wedding, "Do whatever he tells you."

This is a revealing moment. First, it shows that she has some responsibility in the wedding, since the assumption is that the servants must listen to her. Hence the conclusion that this is a wedding of someone from Jesus' family.

Second, it shows how even Mary now responds to Jesus' words with the faith of a disciple, not the fiat of a parent. She recognizes a new time in her son's life is unfolding, and she accepts that change by asserting her faith in his soon-to-be-revealed identity. She is now a follower. The story of the wedding feast in Cana of Galilee is the story of Mary dropping her son off at college; this is Mary watching her son board the bus to boot camp. This is a mother realizing that her role has changed.

Jesus proclaims that his life will unfold according to a divine mission for the revelation of his "hour." And then Jesus, the compassionate son, takes care of the concerns of his mother and the wedding party. He directs the servants to refill the six 20- to 30-gallon water jugs with water and then to draw out that water and serve it to the chief steward, or the caterer, for this wedding event. The result is that this is the best wine that has been served at this important family celebration.

This new wine, 30 Château Jesus, is served at the end of

the wedding celebration, not the beginning. Ernest Hemingway once asserted that wine is "one of the natural things of the world that has been brought to the greatest perfection, and it offers a greater range for enjoyment and appreciation than, possibly, any other purely sensory thing." If he's right, then Jesus got it right the first time he tried. If it's true that the title MW ("Master of Wine") is a scholarly qualification more demanding than most PhDs, then another title for Jesus should be MW.

> **MORE BAD HABITS**
>
> **He might have been a bad investor. Given a relative fortune at birth there is no record of it still being there 30 years later.**
>
> **PETER SCHUMACHER**

The world of wine expertise is a world of its own. The number one wine critic in the world, Robert Parker, insures his nose for $1 million. The world's biggest auction market for top wines is no longer London or New York City but Hong Kong, where three bottles of wine (1869 Château Lafite-Rothschild) recently sold for $230,930 each, and where bottles of Château d'Yquem go for $75,000 each.

In the world of wine, there are bottles of wine and then there are "megabottles." A normal, everyday bottle of wine contains 750 milliliters. Sometimes, at really special occasions or at five-star restaurants, some of us might have seen a *magnum*, an extra-large bottle equivalent to two regular bottles of wine. A magnum is impressive and celebratory.

But there are *much* bigger bottles available to true aficionados. These wine bottles are literally of biblical proportions.

- The Jeroboam is 3,000 milliliters, or the equivalent of four regular bottles of wine.
- The Rehoboam is 4,500 milliliters, or six bottles.
- The Methuselah is 6,000 milliliters, or eight bottles.
- The Nebuchadnezzar is 15,000 milliliters, or twenty bottles.
- The Solomon tops that at 18,000 milliliters, or twenty-four bottles.
- The Melchizedek jumps on the top of the heap with 30,000 milliliters, or forty regular bottles poured into one container.

Unlike giant Costco jars of mustard or vats of pickles, these huge bottles of wine are actually good for the vintage. With a much lower ratio of air to wine, these large containers tend to nurture and produce better wine than their smaller cousins. Sometimes bigger truly is better.

Jesus put his wine into 20- to 30-gallon stone jars, each one a triple Melchizedek. Six jars of this liquid would yield more than 150 gallons of wine—over 560,000 milliliters. This amount was a true superabundance of liquids, of hospitality, and of hosting generosity. And it was deemed "the best." That was a "Jesus" measure of wine. Jesus always leaves leftovers. Jesus always provides a superabundance, a more-than-ever-expected degree of grace.

Currently the best wine in the world is an 1811 Château d'Yquen—a bottle purchased for $120,000 and which the owner claims will be opened and drunk in 2017 (with some foie gras—goose livers—eww!). But the best wine ever made was actually served at a wedding in Cana around 30 CE. And its vintner did not have a great horticultural history.

What do you do with leftovers? Ziploc? Freezer? Trash? Compost? Fat dogs and cats?

In Jesus' day, leftover wines were often put up for auction. Think first-century eBay. All the guests went home, and there were potable, valuable liquids left behind. Why not offer them to the highest bidder? The amount Jesus produced in the final days of this wedding feast suggests that a significant portion would have been left over. Did the bridegroom's family auction off this amazing vintage? After all, it was the best anyone had ever tasted, this 30 Château Jesus, and word of this "Jesus wine" no doubt spread quickly from Galilee to Jerusalem.

Only those with the most resources and influence would have been able to bid on this amazing wine—royalty and the priesthood. Those with the most bid on a wine produced by one with the least. Jesus was a Nazarene, and "nothing good" came out of Nazareth, yet this vintage, this very first of his works, surpassed every other vintage in history. It would make a great novel to tell the story of this wine and where it ended up. Maybe it was the wine that Caiaphas the high priest hoisted to toast the capture of Jesus of Nazareth in the garden of Gethsemane that fateful night. Talk about irony.

We don't know anything else about Jesus' wine. But there are wines that focus on the different kinds of grapes, and there are wines that taste of the place where the grapes were grown and the wine was made. We don't know which kind of wine Jesus made. The latter kind of wines are the most coveted, the wines with *terroir*, a term that denotes an almost mystical combination of soil, climate, weather, grape, winemaking, and winemaker. Some say the French live, breathe, and die for terroir; a wine reflects the whole being of each piece of France. I suspect that Jesus made a wine with terrestrial terroir, a wine that encapsulated what it meant to be human and what it meant to live in harmony on the earth and to bring heaven to earth.

My former doctoral student Mark Chironna notes that "the water only becomes wine when you draw some out." Disciples draw out water, trusting Jesus to turn it into something special, something terrific, something with terroir, something with the whiff of eternity to it.

Jesus had a nose for excellence. That nose for the good, the true, the beautiful only comes from prayer and study and sitting at the feet of Jesus. An 1875 Sercial wine received this rating: "Subdued maybe, but gracious, refined, evocative, and in its way delicious." Not a bad description of those disciples who develop this bad habit of Jesus.

JESUS WAS CONSTANTLY DISAPPEARING

CHAPTER FOUR

JESUS NEVER TRAVELED ALONE. No doubt it would have been easier, and faster, to travel solo. It would have also been easier, and less exasperating, to think silo and organize his life into greater systematic efficiency and effectiveness. But Jesus lived his life in community, with all that comes with the drama and bedlam of human relationships. So Jesus traveled in community and showed how in the midst of the pandemonium of relationships there can be paradise. He formed the first Jesus Seminary and manifested in his life an alternative to living life solo and silo.

But every now and then, especially when things got hectic, Jesus did have the nasty habit of just simply disappearing.

One of my favorite people is artist and pianist Ken Medema. Already nearly blind from birth, Ken began learning to play the piano at age five. Initially able to see shapes and shadows, Ken began less and less to depend upon his eyes to play the piano and more and more upon his senses of hearing and touch. The surer he became, the more he improvised. Although he cannot see the keys, he can feel them. He knows they are there, and he senses in his soul how the music feels to his fingers.

In a sense, our minds go through a similar process when we learn to play an instrument, to type, to ride a bike, to walk. At first, you must have help to learn. You are unsure. Before you put your fingers on the piano keys, you make sure you are centered over middle C. When you are learning to type, you look down to make sure you're seeing the letters *G* and *H* and not some other combination between your index fingers. As you hop onto your bike, you glance down to make sure your foot finds the pedal and your training wheels are holding you in place, or perhaps you look back to make sure your father or mother is behind you with a hand still on the back of the bike, keeping you steady, so you know you won't fall.

Sooner or later, however, you stop looking. Your fingers feel where *F* and *J* are. Your mind and muscles remember. You play a tune not thinking about each note but about the grand melody. You feel the wind on your face and forget to check whether someone is holding on to your bike or not. You dance, lifting your leg into the air, knowing where it needs to go even without the teacher guiding you. You toss salt into your casserole, just the right amount because your fingers remember how much to pinch. You sing in tune and rhythm even when the metronome has stopped.

When you're a child, you allow your parents to hold your hands so you can learn to walk . . . until one day, you find you've done it all by yourself. The hands are gone. But their love and watchful eyes, the remembrance of their hands, are still very much there.

Learning to live in faith, learning to trust Jesus, is like that too. Once you've known him, seen him, touched him, your faith will take over even when the training wheels are gone. And Jesus takes away the training wheels when you least expect it. We may not be children, but we are still children in faith when it comes to Jesus.

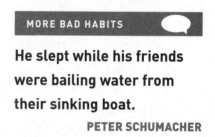

MORE BAD HABITS

He slept while his friends were bailing water from their sinking boat.

PETER SCHUMACHER

Remember when the disciples went out to sea, and Jesus fell asleep in the boat? He disappeared into sleep when the disciples thought they needed him the most—when the wind whipped up and the storm sent the boat rocking and reeling. Or remember when Jesus' disciples left the shore to go home across the water? Jesus disappeared into the cloud-covered mountains, only to join them later by walking across the water. Without his physical presence, when the storms hurled waves over the sides of the boat and the fog made it hard to see, the disciples felt afraid. Their faith was shaken.

Jesus spent his ministry taking off the training wheels and disappearing at the most inopportune moments, preparing his disciples for a time when he would not be with them physically to hold their hand through every storm or to prepare their "syllabus" for what they needed to learn. Jesus knew his disciples would need to know his presence, feel him with them, even when they could not see him. And he made sure they knew he was not deserting them:

> Go and make disciples of all nations, baptizing them in the name of the Father and of the Son and of the Holy Spirit, and teaching them to obey everything I have commanded you. And surely I am with you always, to the very end of the age.[1]

> The Advocate, the Holy Spirit, whom the Father will send in my name, will teach you all things and will remind you of everything I have said to you.[2]

Jesus' disciples got used to him "disappearing," although never for good until the Ascension.

After feeding the five thousand—Jesus disappeared to pray.

After John the Baptist's death—Jesus disappeared to mourn.

After his baptism—Jesus disappeared for forty days and nights before beginning his ministry.

In fact, in the Scriptures, Jesus disappeared from the time

he was twelve until the time he was thirty! You could say Jesus is a master at disappearing and reappearing at the strangest moments!

We can all perhaps say that about ourselves. I know when I was growing up, I was quite good at disappearing when there were chores to be done, only to reappear suddenly at the call to suppertime! But Jesus wasn't disappearing to avoid people so much as to be in touch and in tune with his Father because "the Son can do . . . only what he sees his Father doing."[3]

Jesus' prayer time was not alone time but Father time. He was always escaping into boats, up mountains, to the water, into the desert—anywhere to grab a moment with God. These were not retreats. These were advances. The soul needs two things as a tree needs water and light: solitude and society. Together they form a barbell that the soul lifts to get strong and healthy.

Solitude is not solo time but soul time with God. Solitude is a relationship word, another name for relationship with the self and with the Source. Solitude is not a time-out from relationships, for relationship is central to solitude. Aloneness is not soulful sophistry but sophistication and maturity of relationship with God. A lot of "spiritual problems" are not struggles with God but with self. A lot of mental torments and tossings and turnings of the soul could be solved by a good night's sleep . . . or a good day's diet . . . or a good long walk . . . or a good hug . . . or some deep solitude. But true spiritual struggle needs God-time.

Jesus needed people. As it was "not good" for the first

Adam to be alone, even before the Fall, so it was "not good" for the second Adam to be alone, just before the Cross.[4] Jesus needed other people. We all need people, especially in our lonely hours. Paul confessed that he needed people so much, and knew that he would so enjoy their company, that they might need to kick him out to get him back on the road.[5]

During his last night on earth, Jesus needed both society and solitude: society (companionship of the Last Supper in the upper room) and accompanied solitude (prayer in the garden of Gethsemane), where he was alone but not alone. Gethsemane was a place where olives were pressed to produce the finest oil. Jesus was pressed in prayer—the paradox of human will ("Take this cup from me") struggling with divine will ("Your will be done")—to press for divine forgiveness and favor for humanity and to impress on humanity divine anointing with the oil of healing and health.

We all need the pendulum swing of snatching spaces of solitude and setting tables of sociability. In fact, the more plugged in and connected we are, the more we need to unplug and disconnect. A world of presence needs a time of absence.

Whenever we see Jesus disappear into the wilderness,

> **MORE BAD HABITS**
>
> **After getting a following of folks who were hanging on his every word, he regularly scooted off into the wilderness to be alone . . . with God. Some may have found him antisocial.**
>
> **DAVID TRICKETT**

up a mountain, into a boat, or into a deserted place, it is to take time for deepening his relationship with his Father through prayer and conversation. To advance in solitude is to be renewed by the power of the Holy Spirit and the wisdom of the Father. Every time Jesus reappears after disappearing, something miraculous and majestic happens.

When Jesus disappears into the wilderness for forty days and nights, he reappears to begin his ministry in Cana, where he changes water into the finest wine ever made.

When Jesus disappears into the mountains after feeding the five thousand, he reemerges to walk across the water to his frightened disciples.

When Jesus prays in the garden of Gethsemane for God to remove his "cup," he emerges to walk the road to Calvary and to sing a song of triumph from the agony of the Cross.

Jesus' ultimate disappearing act was his death and burial, and still he reappeared miraculously that Easter morning to Mary at the tomb.

But Jesus' strangest disappearing moments occurred in his post-resurrection appearances. He had told his disciples, "It is for your good that I am going away."[6] And after several disappearing and appearing moments, he sent the Holy Spirit at Pentecost to breathe on us so that we would never be without him and he would be present in and among us in a whole new way.

Each and every time that Jesus disappeared for time alone with God, he returned, renewed and refreshed, to salve our doubts and subdue our fear.

Whether early amid the dimness of dawn, or late amid the darkening of dusk, Jesus' habit of disappearing perhaps was just a dress rehearsal for the time to come, when his disciples would need to be aware of the presence of Jesus even when he appeared absent.

Perhaps this is also the best definition of prayer: the times when we disappear from our busyness and our pressing chores and spend time in God's presence, just as Jesus did. When we reappear from that time with God, what disappears is our doubts, our fears, our inhibitions, our pain. We are refreshed and renewed for another day, and we remember who and whose we are.

The story of Zacchaeus is the paradigm of prayer. "Wee little man" Zacchaeus climbed into a tree in order to see Jesus. He couldn't see Jesus in his own life until he took time out from the crowd and climbed into that sycamore tree. From there, Jesus called him down and called him out. Then Jesus invited himself to Zacchaeus's house for a meal and a relationship. Wherever or whenever or however we find ourselves in prayer, Jesus will find us and invite himself in.

Which is to bring up another bad habit of Jesus—his imposing on others and inviting himself in. Jesus was always borrowing things. He borrowed a boat; borrowed a donkey; borrowed an upper room; borrowed a sepulchre.[7] What parent hasn't taught their kids not to borrow things or invite themselves over to other people's houses? Imposing is rude.

Jesus didn't just invite himself over to Zacchaeus's house. He invited himself over for supper. Jesus inserted himself, riding a donkey, into the "Procession of the Lambs" from Bethlehem to Jerusalem and presented himself as the true Paschal Lamb. An invitation to take a walk or walk alongside someone is an invitation to a certain intimacy in conversation. Jesus invited himself into conversations, like the one on the Emmaus road. And Jesus imposed on several men and women because they were ultimately searching for something that only he could give them. Some encounters were brief; some lasted days. But in each case, Jesus instigated the relationship by imposing upon the one who needed him, whether they knew it at the time or not. Jesus wants his followers to turn imposition into opportunity by seizing it.

Prayer is relational improv. It's knowing Jesus enough to let our faith create our lives anew each and every time we pray. Prayer takes us places we would never think to go. Prayer moves our lives in ways we would never imagine possible. Prayer is less about the words we say than the time we spend in relationship with God.

There is an old Hasidic story about a young Jewish lad who lived on an isolated farm with his family. They were quite poor and lived simple lives. One day the boy got to travel to a village with his father. He was drawn to a synagogue where he heard prayers being recited. His heart was touched, so he went in and sat down to listen to the prayers. The boy was deeply moved and wanted to join in the prayers, but he could not read the siddur, the Hebrew prayer book. So he closed his eyes and simply prayed the alphabet, "Aleph, bet, gimmel, dalet, hey, vav . . ." He recited the alphabet over and over again. Then he said, "O God, I don't know how to pray or what to say. Here are the letters of the alphabet. Use them to make up the prayer I should pray, the words you would like to hear, and answer my prayer as you see fit for me." When we are tired and exhausted and only have enough energy to sing the alphabet, we can trust God to take our groans and sighs and turn them into the prayers God has for us. Whenever we pray, God appears for us, into our lives and into our hearts, and miraculous things happen.

> **MORE BAD HABITS** 💬
>
> **Jesus has a bad habit of doing nothing. He let the rich young ruler go. Today we would be encouraged to pursue such a person.**
>
> **MATTHEW TODD THOMAS**

If we make Jesus' disappearing habit our disappearing habit, we'll be amazed at life's appearances and will discover what poet Louis MacNeice called "the drunkenness of things being various." Prayer is like riding a bike, learning to walk, playing the piano, singing God's praises. The more you do it, the more it becomes second nature. When prayer becomes second nature, your life will look more and more like a beautiful manifestation of Jesus. And you never know when Jesus will appear in your life and something amazing and beautiful and awesome will happen to you.

Frank C. Laubach (1884–1970) was a missionary to the Philippines. He wrote a book on prayer titled *The Mightiest Force in the World* (1946). He was famous for turning prayer first into a disappearing act into someone's life, and second into an imposition: "What are you doing in the world for God that I can help you with?"

The disappearing Jesus is not evidence of a *Deus absconditus* (hidden God) or a *Deus otiosus* (idle God). Jesus disappears in order to be present for us in ways that are fresh and abiding. You cannot make divine presence coincident with the conscious experience of divine presence. There is something more important than a present experience of God—a loving relationship with God that may or may not include a present experience. What made the Holy of Holies so holy was not the Ark, or the art, or the timeless truths engraved in stone but the presence of the living God. When that curtain was cut in two—a new covenant inaugurated by the disappearing of Jesus on the cross—Jesus' presence was poured out for all time on all flesh in every need.

When your best friend shuts the door in your face, Jesus will take you in.

When everyone else leaves the room, Jesus will take you in.

When your employer lets you go, Jesus will take you in.

When your kids want nothing more to do with you, Jesus will take you in.

When everybody fails you, Jesus will take you in.

When everything in life fails you, Jesus will take you in.

Never did someone cry out for help but that Jesus stopped to listen. It is indeed good for us that Jesus went away because now he is with us "always, to the very end of the age."

JESUS OFFENDED PEOPLE, ESPECIALLY IN HIGH PLACES

CHAPTER FIVE

OPRAH HAS SAID that she would have loved to interview Jesus, but I don't think Jesus would have been a good talk-show guest, mainly because of his bluntness. He would have been quickly bounced off the show and labeled as intolerant and offensive. "Easier for a camel to go through the eye of a needle . . ." or "Cast out into outer darkness . . ."[1] He didn't mince words. He called some people "liars," others a "brood of vipers," still others "hypocrites" and "whitewashed tombs."[2] In a flash of anger, he called the most powerful person of his time (Herod) a vicious vulpine.[3] He even called one of his best friends "Satan."[4]

He would probably not even have been let on Oprah's show, because Jesus was always forming unholy alliances with outsiders—with pagans, with pariahs, even with religious terrorists[5]—that offended everyone. Jesus could smell from a mile away the arrogant attitude of "the air is fine up here; how is it down there?" and could launch some preemptive offensive strikes. Or consider perhaps his most intolerant statement of them all: "I am the way."[6]

The tenor of culture has moved from the idea that everyone has a right to their own opinion to the idea that everyone's opinion is equally right. Jesus would not have made many friends with his claims and assertive manner— and he didn't. When Jesus begins citing Scripture, you *know* he's going to nail someone for something.

Sometimes the Prince of Peace was a disturber of the peace so that he could be God's purveyor of true peace—the "peace that passes all understanding," "peace on earth, goodwill to all" peace.

Following Jesus in any culture will be offensive. It was then, and it is now. How do you handle this bad habit of being offensive in a world in which everyone is easily offended or playing defense?

The first line of defense when someone is caught with their moral pants down seems to be Jesus' famous warning against evaluating others—"Judge not!" Why do we feel a need to make judgments on everyone and everything—can't we let God do that? After all, didn't even the pope say, in an off-the-cuff remark about gay priests, "Who am I to judge?"

The words "Don't judge, Sweet" were barked at me on Facebook when I called the Germanwings #9525 copilot who in 2015 crashed his plane into the Alps a "mass murderer." Since he killed over a hundred men, women, children, and infants on board, I posted my thought that this was more than a suicide; this was mass murder. Immediately I was hit by a torrent of rebuke: "Who are you to judge?" and "You can't judge him" and "What gives you the right to call him that?" and "What if he had mental illness?"

I even got the same "Don't judge" response when I condemned ISIS for beheading twenty-one Coptic Christians in Libya in 2015. I touted the massacred Egyptians and Ghanaian as "martyrs." I was told by some in the Christian community, "Sweet, who are you to judge ISIS? You can't judge them. Christians are in no position to judge people of another religion."

> **MORE BAD HABITS**
>
> **Jesus treated outsiders like they were important people, and important people like they were outsiders.**
>
> **NATHAN NORDINE**

Wait a minute. I was taught in school something called critical thinking. I was taught in Sunday school something called ethical judgment. I was taught in theological school something called the gifts of the Spirit—seven of them—one of which is discernment, or right judgment. What do you mean I can't judge?

Did Jesus mean that you and I should never judge? Does anyone get through the day without making judgments?

I also have been reading in my Bible where Jesus is judging all the time. He is making judgments in every story and on every page of the Bible. If you look at Jesus' own life, his personal application often swung from one extreme to another. Some days he appeared as a "hanging judge" right out of a Spaghetti Western. Then on others, Jesus looked as lenient as a justice on the take from an episode of *The Sopranos*.

A million people can't be wrong. A billion people can't be wrong.

Well, yes they can.

Billions of people think women are inferior to men. You know, they're wrong.

Millions of people think human trafficking is okay. You know, they're wrong.

We make unqualified ethical judgments on morality all the time. Slavery is always wrong, absolutely—no?

What Jesus doesn't do is *condemn*. In fact, we are told in John 8 that Jesus never condemned anyone. We are *not* to condemn. Only God can condemn.

I am so glad God sees the whole video of my life and not just the snapshot of where I am now. The worst of me no more defines who I am than the worst of Christians defines Christianity. I hope one day God will judge me by my best, not my worst. And the one who will one day judge me is the one who did the most to save me and show me how much God loves me.

But for daily living, we need critical discernment, moral

judgment, and compassionate evaluation of what brings life and what brings death.

One of the worst things you can say about Jesus is that he didn't offend anyone. Jesus—inoffensive? As the dog complained to its master, "When you say, 'Don't worry, he doesn't bite,' do you know how that makes me feel?" Jesus is the greatest offense who ever lived. He was "pierced for our transgressions"[7]—and his offensiveness. And for the church to go on offense, and not just play defense, it must be willing to offend as well. In fact, things we commonly say, like "Are you ready for Christmas?" need to be understood for just how offensive they are. No one ever has been, or ever will be, ready for a world-changing Messiah. But we can be open to receive the revolution.

What Jesus also didn't do was wear his emotions on his sleeve. I brought my kids up with a mantra: Don't litter your food; don't litter your mood. In Edward Docx's *Self Help*, one of the most interesting (and hideous) characters, Nicholas, loses his patience with the annoying Isabella in a way we all can cheer:

> You seem to think just because you feel a thing,
> that makes it externally true. You . . . seem to live
> at the mercy of whatever juvenile emotions you are
> suffering. And please don't kid yourself, Isabella.
> Because in this you're just like all the others out
> there, all the earnest young women scraped into
> the polytechnics . . . heads stuffed full of daytime

TV and magazines, all the whining Princess Diana housewives who have conveniently forgotten how thick they were at school and how thick they continue to be. . . . Just because you aren't intelligent enough to do anything but feel, you want the rest of us to live within the tyranny of whatever the insecurity of the day might be.[8]

Everyone seems to have some chip on their shoulder, quick to take offense or to expect others to toe lines of their own creation. But remember: the place where offense is most easily taken is in prison. Those most irritated by someone else's "offenses" are insecure, insolent people, not mature, cultured people.[9] We live in a world where people are running around, not with chips on their shoulders but the whole tree, or even the entire forest.

Jesus wasn't afraid of saying and doing things that stirred up sensibilities and conflicted with political correctness. It used to be that morality and conscience provided the compass for correct behavior. Now politics provide the compass, or at least something

> **MORE BAD HABITS**
>
> **Jesus put people in uncomfortable positions, asking questions people could not answer, or the questions made them so uncomfortable that they were unwilling to face what they knew was the answer.**
>
> **RAY NEU**

called "political correctness," a dogma that elevates not giving offense as the summum bonum. Actor Charlton Heston
put it well: "Political correctness is tyranny with manners."

The tyranny of PC czars is one reason why there is a
growing sullenness and sourness to our culture. There is an
update to Mae West's complaint "It's hard to be funny when
you have to be clean." It's hard to be funny when you have to
be PC. In fact, it's more than hard. It's downright impossible.

The tyranny of PC czars is also why it is so hard to have
a real, authentic conversation anymore. Political correctness
makes language into a political minefield and turns conversations into duologues, not dialogues.

A duologue is a conversation in which no one is listening.
Our conversations on race, for example, have been almost
exclusively high-pitched, shouting duologues, not attentive,
respectful dialogues. What comes out of mouths in a duologue is a projectile, laser guided to its target by unabashed
political and moral correctitude aimed to shut down, not
open up, conversation. No wonder black-white conversations are either hubs of hatred or hammocks of evasions and
equivocations.

When political correctness takes over in the church, it's
no longer about Jesus. It's placating-interest-groups theology. The gospel becomes not God's Good News but our
own good intentions. The soteriology of the PC-compliant
church is based on "What were your intentions?" If they line
up and are PC compliant, then voilà!—we're saved, although
there is no "salvation" language, only applause and inclusion

and confirmation of our goodness. And once again, intention ends up being all about works. Works without faith in Christ.

The best argument against the rectitude of political correctitude is 1 John 3:18: "Dear children, let us not love with words or speech but with actions and in truth." We spend so much time and energy loving with our language that we have little time and energy left to love "in truth and actions." Or as Danish philosopher Søren Kierkegaard begins one of his essays, "These are Christian reflections; therefore they are not about love but about the works of love."[10]

Every thought does not need to be clothed in cotton. The gospel does not need to be gorged in goose down. The way of Jesus is a way out of the rat race in economics (where it seems to be a requirement to step on others to get ahead) as well as in politics (where it seems to be a requirement to lie in good faith).

Jesus' bad habit of not being afraid to offend so offends our PC sense of rectitude that he would be liable to be arrested for indecency. Consider the plight of Yvette Bavier, the sixty-year-old New Yorker who a few years back was arrested for littering. Her offense? She was feeding sparrows on her lunch break in Central Park West.

Offensiveness, like beauty, is in the eyes of the beholder. We will not mean to offend. But we will.

Nearly eight hundred years ago, Thomas Aquinas, the church's greatest theologian, lamented that we had no name for the virtue of anger in our religious lexicon. He quoted the words of John Chrysostom to make his point: "Whoever is without anger, when there is cause for anger, sins."[11] Jesus offended people with multiple anger episodes: when he saw how people were treating children, when he saw how a tree was hoarding its resources for itself and not feeding a hungry world, and when he saw a sacred courtyard turned into a stockyard and stock exchange.

This last Temple tantrum gave such offense, it proved the last straw for the religious establishment. To the casual observer, Jesus completely lost it. He went off on the guys working in the Temple. I mean, he put a

MORE BAD HABITS

Had trouble getting some things right—like figuring out who the "righteous" people were.

MARY SHAMSHOIAN

beat-down on them that they did not soon forget. He called them robbers and thieves. But from whom did they steal and what did they take that got Jesus so hot under the tunic? I don't think it was money; rather, they stole the grandeur away from God by serving the institution rather than God. They turned a house of prayer into a house of profit. When people today work for the church instead of working for God, love a denomination more than they love God, cherish their traditions more than they cherish their relationship with God, then they steal what is due only God. And I bet Jesus still gets angry—not angry *at* us but angry *over* us. "Sinners in the Hands of an Angry God" may be the most famous sermon in US history, but God is not angry at us. As the fourteenth-century mystic Julian of Norwich pointed out, "If God were angry with us even for a moment, then we would cease to exist."[12] But God does get angry at our lack of offense at how we treat each other.

There is only one passage where Jesus is said to get angry directly. But his anger at their "hardened hearts" leads him to heal.[13] This is not the ale and testosterone raging of today's road rage, home rage, work rage, political rage, or religious rage. Jesus' anger is righteous outrage.

Weddings have made famous the thirteenth chapter of Paul's first letter to the Corinthians. And the reader usually lingers lovingly over the phrase that love "is not easily provoked."[14] But this is a terrible translation. First, the word "easily" is not in the Greek but added by the translators. Second, the actual Greek word we translate as "provoked" is *paroxynetai*, the root of which gives us the word "paroxysm" or more popularly "fit." Love does not issue in "fits"—fits of despair, fits of anger, fits of hopelessness, or fits of selfishness. But love *is* provoked, and love *is* provocative. In fact, that's the very meaning of love, to be provoked by suffering and injustice and inhumanity. To follow Jesus is to be provoked . . . and provocative.

If we are to live out Christ in the world, we need to get rid of our fear of offending people and get on with Christ's mission in the world.

JESUS TOLD STORIES THAT DIDN'T MAKE SENSE

CHAPTER SIX

JESUS HAD A BAD HABIT of turning stories into life and life into stories. But most of the time, when he told his stories, the majority of his listeners had no clue what he was talking about. Or just when they thought they knew where he was going, his ending confounded them. Or even more maddening, he let *them* end it. Jesus often left the last word on what he meant to those who heard the story.

Jesus' stories are the original "shock and awe." If you hear one of Jesus' stories and your jaw isn't dropping while your stomach is churning, your bones rattling and your mind reeling, you've missed the best part of the story!

Jesus was master of the trick metaphor and twist ending. He would come up with a metaphor that everyone knew, and once they were drawn into the story and felt comfortable . . . *pow!* All of a sudden, the story took a twist, and the ending left people confounded, confused, dazed, and shocked.

Consider the story Jesus tells of the rich man and Lazarus.[1] In Jesus' day, everyone listening would think they knew where the story was going. The rich man was pretty good, already allowing a leper to park just outside his gate—and feeding him, no less. But Jesus teaches that even this is not enough. We aren't meant just to hand out things to people but to be in relationship with people! It's the difference between working at a soup kitchen and befriending your poor neighbors and inviting them into your home for dinner, as you would anyone else. Jesus had significant shock value no matter what he taught. The answer was never what was expected.

> **MORE BAD HABITS**
>
> **He had the bad habit of not answering direct questions.**
>
> **FELIX FERNANDEZ**

A typical Jesus story or parable was atypical for his day. It didn't leave people with a conclusion but made them draw one on their own. And it would never be the obvious one. A parable by definition undermines the status quo; it doesn't reinforce it.

The most important part of any story is the missing piece. And Jesus had a bad habit of answering questions with either questions or stories. If stories, they were stories that either didn't make immediate sense, confused people, or were full of missing pieces that the listener had to jigsaw in.

Jesus' teaching runs against the grain, then and now. A Jesus story is as pitiless as a migraine. So if a Jesus story isn't giving you a headache or plaguing you with sleepless nights as you turn it over and over, you'll need to reread until it does.

Jesus' mysterious, open-ended, twisty endings were brilliantly conceived, and his lack of explanation was perfectly pitched. He wanted people not only to think about the story and to converse with each other about the story, but also to ask him about the story. Ultimately, Jesus' stories are about cultivating a relationship with him. We call it *discipleship*.

Jesus' stories were about relationships—not power relationships but human relationships, specifically the abundant-life relationship with God, oneself, each other, and creation. And if it took a bit of perplexity to drive people to want to know more, Jesus was all for it, even if it meant he was frequently misunderstood. Even if it meant he would be attacked for those misunderstandings.

Why Jesus constantly opens himself to being misunderstood remains a mystery. When he identifies himself as the Prince of Peace who comes bringing a sword, he is referring to the violence of cutting, the conflict of cutting apart, but also to cutting as a surgeon cuts to heal the conflicts in societies, in families, in one's own self. Or when Jesus tells his disciples that two swords will be enough for them,[2] he is not presenting himself as "Rabbi Rambo" but is instructing his disciples that, along with the purse and bag and sandals they will need, well, two swords should be enough to stem off the attackers who will want to kill them. Jesus is a revolutionary, not of any political movement, but of a dynamic prophetic movement designed to bring all humanity back into relationship with God. He is endowed with God's power, a catalyst more powerful than any politics. But he could only be a catalyst to those who sought to dig deeper for his meanings. Jesus spoke to whoever followed him. But Jesus taught those who sought a relationship with him.

A lot of people followed Jesus around. Some were drawn into his magnetic field because they thought he was charismatic, intriguing, eccentric, and compelling. They wondered what he'd do next. Some of them no doubt fed off his style of pushing the envelope. Some undoubtedly lived just to see another confrontation between Jesus and the Temple authorities. A crowd always gathers to see the school-yard fight.

Others came for the food! Jesus had another habit of handing out food when he taught for several hours. The Messiah liked to eat. Why not hang out and fill the stomach? A picnic on the hillside might be just right.

Some were really interested in what this provocative rabbi had to say. He certainly had different ideas. And he told the best stories. He related those stories to everyday things everyone could understand—farming, masonry, baking, shepherding—even while he made the familiar strange. So what if his stories didn't completely make sense? They left you thinking. And there was often a lesson or two to catch if you thought long enough.

But the people Jesus was interested in the most, the ones Jesus celebrated the most, were those who asked questions like he did. If you take something seriously, you ask questions. Those who took Jesus seriously were the ones who wanted to know more. The ones who wanted to know why the stories took strange trajectories. The ones most willing to be taught. Jesus loved people who would not just listen to him, but who would follow him, learn from him, and be in relationship with him—and with God.

> **MORE BAD HABITS** 💬
>
> **Forgot to explain "the moral of the story is" when commending the shrewd manager in Luke 16.**
>
> **JIM HENDERSON**

We think the question of life is "Where are you, God?" when the real question of life is God asking us every day and every way, as God asked Adam and Eve, "Where are *you*?" What is the first question asked in the New Testament? The Magi ask, "Where is the one who has been born king of the Jews?"[3] We are on a hunt for something that is already present.

Jesus was not averse to getting in other people's faces with his questioning. Jesus could be nosy, always asking questions to pry his way into other people's lives. I once told some youth the story of Jesus meeting the Samaritan woman at the well. Jesus told the woman that he knew she had been married five times and was living with some guy right then. I then asked the teens what this meant, and one girl announced, "It means

Jesus got all up in her business!" She was right. Jesus regularly "got all up in" people's business. In fact, the whole story of the Incarnation is the story of God, not born of alphabets and words but born of a virgin, who became flesh and got all up in the human business.

But the ones who had Jesus in their business the most were those in his inner circle—for whom every story was a conversation, a deeper dig into the Scriptures to find those missing pieces. The pearls of great price. The diamonds in the dust.

The best gifts are used items, heirlooms haloed with memories, artifacts stuffed with stories. Everything Jesus said and did was stuffed with story—the story of Scripture. His ability to link memory and imagination, to reveal the beauty and depth and hidden meanings of Scripture, was laser sharp and brilliant.

Playwright David Hare gave this evaluation of Jesus' storytelling: "Jesus Christ was prone to making comments which seem to support an almost infinite variety of exegesis. A remark like 'Render unto Caesar the things that are Caesar's and unto God the things that are God's' could almost have been produced by computer scientists working at the cutting edge of linguistic theory to formulate the single human sentence responsible to the greatest imaginable number of readings."[4]

Jesus spoke in parables deliberately. He was interested in something much more than mere clarity of thought and a routine answer. He didn't teach in order for someone to learn the right response. His teaching was not a mere cerebral exercise. He taught so that the soul would be surprised into experiencing a new, authentic revelation of truth, one that would pour over into life and living. For that, Jesus needed to slow down reception and infuse an element of participation—and a dose of doubt.

While his stories sounded simple and at first easy, they quickly evoked a quizzical response. The initial reaction might be: *Smile. How great!* But then after a short pause: *Wait, what?*

Jesus sounded enigmatic. He was a confusing conversationalist. He would answer a question with a question, talk in circles, and often change the subject altogether. Almost ambiguous, his puzzling statements frustrated even his closest followers. His every answer seemed to be shrouded in mystery. Why? Because Jesus was communicating immortal truths to mortal minds—eternal truths to flesh and blood. He knew what information they could handle, and most important, when they needed to handle it. He led his followers down illuminated paths of enlightenment and spoon-fed them the next necessary tidbits of information, all the while maintaining his intention for a total revelation of truth. As he continues to use this process today, Jesus' followers must know that he welcomes our honest questions, and we can trust his responses even when we don't fully understand them.

In John's Gospel, Jesus asked the brothers James and John, "What do you want?" They said, "Rabbi, where are you staying?" And Jesus replied, "Come and see."[5] The question

"Where are you staying?" was more than "What's your e-mail?" or "How can we reach you?" or "Can I have your address?" It meant "How can we learn from you, Rabbi, so that we find our true home?" Jesus doesn't answer his disciples with an easy answer: "Here's where you can reach me." He answers them with an invitation: "Join me and journey with me and learn from me—with your whole body, mind, and spirit." There is no neutral gear in the gospel of Jesus—only full commitment to the Story will do.

When you're in the middle of a Jesus story and you think, *So far, so good*, you're in the wrong story. When you're in the middle of a Jesus story and you think, *So far, so odd*, you're in the right story. Sam Proctor used to say the key to preaching was to get Jesus in so much trouble in the first part of your sermon that no one believes it's possible to get him out of it. He said it was pretty easy to do if you gave the Gospels an honest reading.

The ancient rabbis exhorted Jews studying the Torah to "turn it over, turn it over, because everything is inside of it." First you "open" the Story, then you "turn it over, turn it over." There is a Story—turn, turn, turn. It is the turn of the Story that turns lives back to God. This bad habit of Jesus will lead us to never underestimate the power of story to cultivate the imagination and change the heart. We don't just read the stories of the Bible; we live in them, and they live in us.

Even if Jesus were not the Son of God, just his stories alone would make him famous as history's greatest storyteller.

The better the storytelling, the more Jesus the church. When the church stops being a storehouse of stories and becomes a treasure house of silver and gold, points and props, it ceases to be the body of Christ.

Story is the flesh and blood of life. And the body of Christ needs to be fed with the stories of the gospel—stories that shock and stories that twist around our self-concerned notions and expectations and leave us naked, confused, witless, and willing to let God lead us into new pastures. Today's churches need more of Jesus' storytelling habit. When a church is fed only points and propositions, rules and answers, it's like a body nourished on husks and shells. Without propositions, it's like trying to stand up without a skeleton . . . but propositions and principles come from the stories, not stories from the propositions.

If truth be nothing more than propositions and principles, the Bible would be one long list of dos and don'ts.

You can't escape living in and through a story. All of us are living a story. The question is what story and whose story are you living? Madison Avenue? Wall Street? Hollywood? Or Bethlehem?

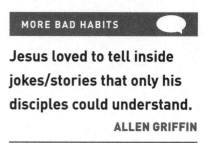

MORE BAD HABITS

Jesus loved to tell inside jokes/stories that only his disciples could understand.

ALLEN GRIFFIN

The Bible is not a "Once upon a time," tooth-fairy storybook but an "In the beginning," true-grit storybook. Jesus' stories were made for life in all of its messiness, grittiness, pain, and confusion.

God made humans with an inner valve that creaks and groans, shakes and drips until opened to disclose one's state of being, the story of one's soul.

The Greatest Story Ever Told was made to resonate God in the echoes of our souls. Faith is not "to live as if the Story is true." Faith is to stake your whole life on the knowledge that the Story *is* true.

With Jesus' bad habit of turning everything into a story, here is a prayer to use upon opening the Bible: "As I enter your Story, may your Story enter me that as I enter your world, your Story may enter through me."

JESUS LOVED TO PARTY

CHAPTER SEVEN

IF THEY'D HAD PAPARAZZI back in the first century, Jesus would have been in a lot of their pictures. He would have gotten past the velvet rope at any club in town. He was in high demand as a guest. Why?

Because Jesus was the life of every party. So much so that less-than-kosher people often hosted VIP events for him, causing the religious establishment to label him a party animal. Are his followers today too stuffy? Have we missed all the fun? Should we loosen up and belly up to the salad bar? Are we missing golden opportunities to influence popular culture because we are afraid to be seen having fun? Jesus teaches us that the party habit could be the best way to break the ice and influence even the seediest of characters.

Not only that, but we know from Scripture that God throws a party whenever one of his lost comes home. God promised the Israelites a land of milk and honey, a place of fruitfulness and plenty. The Kingdom of Heaven is portrayed in the Scriptures as a festival and feast with a place for everyone at God's table of abundance.

> **MORE BAD HABITS**
>
> **Jesus drank a lot of wine, walked away from fights, invited himself for dinner (and brought uninvited guests!).**
>
> **MARGARET TERRY**

Even the imagery of the Garden is a place of abundant food and drink. God favors Abel's roasted lamb and delights in the smell of barbecue. And when Israel praised the Lord, they offered food, song, dance, and music.

No wonder the Son of God loves eating and drinking so much! Far from the asceticism of John the Baptist, Jesus had a habit of making the best wine and delighting in banquets at which he was accused many times of eating with sinners.

In fact, if you know anything about Jesus' bad habits of "eating and drinking,"[1] you might wonder what Macarius of Alexandria, or Serapion, or Pachomius, or Finnchua, or Ite, or Ciarán, or Kevin were thinking as disciples of Jesus, since their habits are a far cry from Jesus' party habit. These later "disciples" did things like eating no cooked food for seven years; or spending seven years suspended by the armpits from iron shackles; or remaining in a standing posture for seven years; or mixing bread with sand; or sleeping naked in a marsh for six months, exposing the skin to poisonous flies and other creatures; or not going horizontal to sleep for forty or fifty years, never speaking a word, carrying heavy weights wherever they went, living in iron bracelets and chains . . . all of them competing in the marathon of extreme asceticism. These are some of our favorite saints!

Benedict of Nursia is most often depicted with a bundle of switches in his right hand. Most famous of all, though, was Simeon Stylites, who started off living on a six-foot perch in the Syrian desert but then was ashamed of being such a slacker, so he built a sixty-foot-high perch that was three feet across, where he spent more than thirty years exposed to the elements. A ladder brought up buckets of food and brought down buckets of waste. The rope he tied himself to so he wouldn't fall became a part of his body, like a chain wrapped tight around a tree, except the tree accepts the chain but his flesh rejected the rope, and the stench of putrid flesh could be smelled from a long way off. When the worms that lived in the infection fell off, Simeon would replace them, saying, "Eat what God has given you." Even our favorite saint, Francis of Assisi, whom we adore for his love of

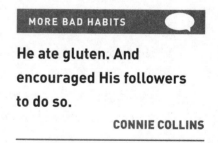

MORE BAD HABITS

He ate gluten. And encouraged His followers to do so.

CONNIE COLLINS

animals and gentle nature, still sprinkled ashes like salt into his food for fear he would enjoy it too much.

Why do we feel that to be good and faithful Christians, we must not look too happy, not enjoy ourselves too much, when throughout the Scriptures, God clearly loves a party?

The church plays the music of Jesus in mostly minor keys. But the Bible's symphonic stories have major-key, blue-sky sound tracks with minor-key, blues moments. But the dissonant moments always resolve into beautiful harmonies in God's grand symphony. Jesus was a "man of sorrows, and acquainted with grief,"[2] and there is a place for sorrow and grief in the life of faith. After all, there is a book of Lamentations in the Bible. Everyone has sorrows in life. The question is not "Will we have sorrows?" but "Will we be a 'waster of sorrows'?"[3]

> **MORE BAD HABITS** 💬
>
> **Jesus chose to befriend someone from the tax department!**
>
> **RICHARD GIVEN**

But even in the middle of this book of trials and tribulations there is a promise, in the words of the psalmist, "to declare Your lovingkindness in the morning and Your faithfulness by night."[4] In the midst of a book that chronicles every lamentable situation imaginable, there is one of the greatest declarations of joy and hope you'll find anywhere: "But this I call to mind, and therefore I have hope: The steadfast love of the LORD never ceases; his mercies never come to an end; they are new every morning; great is your faithfulness."[5]

We don't know much about the apostolic age. What we do know is that they ate. They ate together . . . a lot! And it was no doubt the joy of their day.

Hedonism—the belief that happiness is the goal of life—has a bad rap in the church, not because pleasure is bad, but because we have a wrong perception, a crude conception of pleasure as somehow being selfish or not solemn enough to honor Jesus.

"Delight sets the soul in its place," Augustine maintained in his early handbook on Latin meter. And in his commentary on Galatians, he said, "We necessarily act in accordance with what delights us more."[6] Our hope is one of an eternity of pleasure, not an eternity of suffering and deprivation.

Go ahead, follow Joseph Campbell's advice and "Follow your bliss." But be forewarned: in God alone is there a life of true bliss, a life of pure pleasure.

I am never happier than when weary of body and exhausted of spirit after a full, long day of preaching, teaching, and serving. Can I get a witness to the joys of sentness and spentness? My friend Teri Hyrkas, in a book review for preachthestory.com, said,

When Jesus and the disciples were at the well in Samaria, the disciples were so worried about Jesus' exhaustion and hunger that they left him alone and went to find food. When they got back, after Jesus' astonishing visit with the Samaritan woman, the disciples urge him to eat, but he says "I have food to eat that you know nothing about." The disciples are perplexed—did someone else bring him food? Jesus tells them, "My food is to do the will of him who sent me and to finish his work." Eating the bread of heaven is filling and satisfying.

Jesus took great delight in giving delight and in delighting in life.

The Greek word *eudaimonia* means the "summum bonum of the human condition." It means living well and flourishing in all aspects of existence. If anyone was a eudaemonist, it was Jesus. Jesus took great delight in the beauty of God's existence and loved to celebrate God's blessings in the company of others. For Jesus, life was all about relationships, especially God's relationship with his people. Humankind was meant to live an abundant life in relationship with God, who fills us and frees us.

> *You make known to me the path of life;*
> *in your presence there is fullness of joy;*
> *at your right hand are pleasures forevermore.*
> PSALM 16:11, ESV

In the film business, right after a movie finishes shooting, there's a gathering called a wrap party (as in, "It's a wrap," meaning it's finished). The church needs more wrap parties to celebrate the "finishing" of God's plan for all people. For Christians, every day is a reminder of the Resurrection. Each and every day should be a grand celebration of God's amazing gift of Jesus. Everything in life is filled with resurrection moments. And every person is filled with resurrection hope just waiting to be celebrated.

The church above all should be a place of festivities and joy. People should look at the church and think, *What joyful people!* If more of the church shared Jesus' bad habit of loving to party, it would be the place everyone would want to be.

JESUS COULD BE
DANGEROUS

CHAPTER EIGHT

AS AN INFANT, he spooked a king.

As a child, he shocked the theologians.

As an adult, he confounded the powers that be, and he startled everyone.

Jesus had a bad habit of coming across as dangerous.

The television show *Deadliest Catch* on the Discovery Channel is about crab fishing in the Bering Sea. The narrator always says something dramatic like "Out here you are only a moment away from disaster" or "One wrong move could be their last." As theatrical as that sounds, in Alaska, it is a reality.

We all need to learn the relationship between real faith

that can put us into dangerous situations and the real danger of misinterpreting the Scriptures to our own advantage. Wrong interpretations can yield pharisaical commitment to practices and rituals rather than to the person of Jesus. But true faith that walks the talk and toes the line of true discipleship can be downright dangerous. This is the line that Jesus regularly walked, and it is the same line that he still calls his followers to find and walk today. Jesus really scared people. When was the last time you made a faith choice that frightened anyone, yourself included? Is your faith too safe? The path of discipleship can be dangerous and circuitous. Lasting change in anyone's life is seldom a straight line. It's most often a series of zigzags, U-turns, and roundabouts. Faith is not a synonym for fail-safe.

Jesus was curious about many things, always exploring, trying out new approaches, adventurously embracing and meeting with new people who weren't part of his entourage and enclave. For his day, Jesus thought crazy and talked crazy, and he acted as he thought and talked. Or as the cliché of the day would put it, Jesus "got out over his skis." Which means, people thought he was dangerously unrealistic.

Jesus didn't want to change just the Temple or the way people did things in Jerusalem. He didn't want people to change just a few habits. Jesus wanted them to change *everything*—mind, heart, and soul. He didn't want to just make a difference in the world; he wanted to make a different world.

How crazy is that?

Jesus imagined a world of untold possibilities for people

who were used to being kept in pens of cultural constrictions. It is one thing to return love for love. Jesus invited people to imagine a "turn-of-the-cheek" world where people would return love for hate, forgiveness for betrayal, compassion for rejection, passion for indifference, embrace for neglect.

> ### MORE BAD HABITS 💬
>
> **He has a bad habit of stepping on my toes.**
>
> **HOLLY BOARDMAN**

And Jesus exemplified what he expressed, to the point of putting his life not just on the line but on the cross.

The danger of global digitization is that it drains away the blood and reduces the world to flat ones and zeros. The danger of Jesus discipleship is that it pumps so much blood that it enlarges the world to horizons of beauty and blessing that sometimes appear frightening to those penned behind pent-up hopes and dreams. Jesus has the bad habit of shoving a mirror in your face so that you can actually see how beautiful God made you and how much better the way of following him is. In the midst of your indignity, whatever it is, Jesus bestows dignity. He has the bad habit of seeing the good in others.

The "Nice God" of therapeutic culture leads one to expect that if I have a need, God needs to meet my need. This is Christianity as Niceianity. For Jesus, God is loving and merciful and true but not necessarily "nice." The Holy God is dangerous, because the Holy God is Truth. And Jesus had an annoying habit of bringing truth up and taking truth seriously.

Jesus bummed out the intellectuals and theologians of his day because he chilled to intellectual pursuits and theological trappings. Jesus didn't dream of carrying away the glittering prize of philosophy. The problem with intellectualism is that it makes knowledge, not love, foundational. Or as Albert Camus put it, "An intellectual is someone whose mind watches itself." Jesus, by contrast, had a mind and spirit that watched what God was doing so that he could find ways to help humans *join* what God was doing. And the truth business God was (and is) in is the relationship business.

The Greek historian Thucydides wrote in the fifth century BCE, "The first casualty of war is truth." If we are constantly at war, how profound are the casualties? You can be in danger because you know too little, and you can be in danger because you know too much. That's why Jesus was always telling stories and showing signs—because of their truth content. Stories and signs don't lack truth value; they lock in truth value. Truth for Jesus was timelessness made timely by the time-full. And to live relational truth is dangerous in a world of philosophical truth.

The southern cassowary is reputed to be the most dangerous bird on earth. I say the dove is the most dangerous bird on earth. Why? The dove is the symbol of the Holy Spirit, and allowing the Holy Spirit of Jesus Christ to come into your life and change it can feel very, very dangerous. The sign of the dove is poetic code for "live dangerously." It is dangerous to be led by the Spirit and live the stories of Jesus. They're like a virus that you catch quickly and can't get rid of—or a mustard seed that grows rapidly and rampantly. To follow Noah's dove to unknown future places is to disrupt the normal patterns of your life, disturb the comfortable patterns of your world, and explore new landscapes and chart new territory. Like the Magi, who found themselves in danger when searching for Jesus, you travel by a different route when you ride on the wings of the Spirit. You change your plans, choose new paths, go forward by another way, and in doing so become a sign for others on their journeys.

The truth is, doves are really pigeons—homing pigeons, carrier pigeons, sky rats. The sign of the Holy Spirit is a messy, common bird. But the carrier pigeon is a homing pigeon. Traveling with Jesus is not always dignified, pretty, or easy. Jesus takes the common routes and dangerous pathways, seeks out the messy and the dirty and the difficult. But traveling with Jesus is also beautiful, for those who follow Jesus also bring God's lost and dirty people home to God— to be renewed, to be cleansed, to be clothed, to be loved.

Jesus was dangerous to the religious establishment because he taught a faith, not a religion. Jesus was dangerous to anything that came between us and God, which made Jesus especially dangerous to religious professionals. How often does our "religion" get between us and God? Are we so filled up with religion and all its trappings that there isn't room for the inpourings of God's presence and the outpourings of God's power? Jesus was dangerous to all who see faith not as a walk and a way but as a theological edifice made of marble with solid granite foundations, a superstructure of theological boulders towering high and imposing after centuries of building theological statements.

Jesus was willing to embrace what scares us most in life—disturbances, disruptions, discordance, contradictions, oppositions, uncertainties, unpredictability—which are life's primary sources of creativity. He even gave his disciples a sacrament of failure, the sacramental shuffle, to keep them moving when they were rejected or dejected—"shake the dust off your feet."[1] Jesus is the way *into* a life of truth, not a way *out of* life's problems, difficulties, failures, and missteps. Jesus' way makes it possible to live through life's difficulties and turn those difficulties into a testimony, because when we go through them, we deepen our faith, now tested, now proven, now known, and now able to be shared.[2]

Who can ever forget those three space-shuttle astronauts in the first three-man space walk ever? They caught with their gloved hands a 4.5-ton satellite spinning out of control in the wrong altitude. So what enabled the three astronauts to risk everything to restore a satellite? It was some foot restraints that anchored them to the mother craft. We may need to take some "space walks" in our lives to correct some wrong altitudes and attitudes. But we can take the risks of a space walk only if we have some foot restraints that anchor us in the faith and tie us to the Holy Spirit.

If followers of Jesus really fell in love with Jesus and really followed him, we'd be dangerous—and *contagious*. When John the Baptist first met Jesus when both were yet unborn, John "shouted" or "leaped for joy" in his mother's womb.[3]

When our hearts start dancing and shouting for joy in the presence of Jesus, the church will be contagious and dangerous again. The next place Jesus goes after he gets in our hearts is to get under our skin.

Life is both a quest and a pilgrimage—a quest of dreams, but a pilgrimage in which the pilgrim is constantly being changed and so too are the dreams. Can we ditch old dreams and hitch new hopes to imaginative horizons that find their home in the dangerous habits of Christ? It's the only way for us to be dangerous and contagious again.

We live in a culture where truth does not matter. All that matters are the symbols and the opinions we set our agendas upon. In fact, that's all that's left—my opinion and your opinion, equally valid and true.

The church is now even mirroring the culture, more fixated on rights than right. It is hard to speak truth, whether in love or in anger, when the very concept of truth is in crisis. But the church loses its way when it forgets that what it's about has something to do with truth and that what's at stake is nothing less than

MORE BAD HABITS

[He] constantly put the disciples in danger.

ALLEN GRIFFIN

everything, even life itself. The ultimate heresy is the reduction of truth to an opinion. In order to lie, one must be acquainted with the truth. In order to be damned, one must be acquainted with what it means to be saved. In order to be truthful, you have to constantly admit that you can never tell the whole truth—you don't know it, and you don't own it. In fact, something can be partly true but dangerously false, depending on how and when it is said. But you can move from the shadows into the greater light of truth. John Henry Newman and his close friend Ambrose St. John shared a tombstone with this inscription, written by Newman: "*Ex umbris et imaginibus in veritatem*"—"From shadows and images into truth."

Jesus was a dangerous challenger of the truth and a harsh revealer of the truth of God's love and mercy in the world. With every healing, every touch, every challenge, and every forgiving word, Jesus revealed the truth of God.

The Light of the World is truth. In a tiny bundle, God wrapped truth in love. Jesus enters our hearts and beckons us to the loftiest heights and beyond the farthest reaches of the human spirit.

We have no message that brings light and life to the world. We preach not what, but who. "O Come, O Come Emmanuel"—God *with* us. When we live with "withness," dangers become dreams, not daggers.

Alfred North Whitehead argued (persuasively, as far as I'm concerned) that a certain doctrine "should be looked upon as one of the greatest intellectual discoveries of the history of religion." He traced this "doctrine" to Plato in the *Sophist* and *Timaeus*, and here is the doctrine: the divine element in the world is a persuasive and not a coercive agency. But this doctrine is actually found in the Hebrew religion first and reaffirmed by Jesus.

Paul got that doctrine down to one word. One of Paul's favorite words is three little letters in English: *let*. "Let the word of Christ dwell in you richly"[4] and "Let this mind be in you, which was also in Christ Jesus."[5] The word is *let*. Not agonize, beg, or strive. The word is *let*. "Let it be to me," Mary said, "according to your word."[6] Miracles happen when you *let*—when you say, "Let it be to me" and "Let it be me." When you live dangerously and say to God the word "Let . . . Jesus live in me!"

JESUS HUNG OUT WITH BAD PEOPLE

CHAPTER NINE

JESUS HAD THE BAD HABIT of liking people who were not like others and whom others did not like. In fact, some of them were downright unlikable. Even demonic.[1]

Jesus not only liked them, he went out of his way to find them, just like he went out from his heavenly home to find us—to seek, to save, and to love us. *All* of us. Even those who least deserve it. This bad habit, more than any other, cost him his life. Jesus made friends of "sinners" and enemies of "the saints" of his day.

That Jesus befriended bad people (unlike many in religious bubbles) meant that his relational DNA touched as many diverse cells, so to speak, as possible. Jesus was a network thinker, and from the most recent literature on the power of networks, "our human connections with others are in effect an extension of the way our brain interacts with the world."[2] Humans are social organisms whose growth depends on the breadth and width of relational networks. The more our relationships are linked socially and emotionally with diverse others, the richer and fuller life will be.

If there's anything that bothered the Pharisees in Jesus' day, it's that Jesus hung out with people who were considered "unclean" by the lawmakers' rules. Jesus had impure relational networks.

Jesus read the woman at the well's mail: "The man you are now living with isn't your husband."[3] Here was a Samaritan woman who had been manhandled five times. Since a woman couldn't divorce her husband and only males could initiate divorce, here was a "bad" girl who had been used by five men and then dumped when (most likely) she proved barren. In the first century, failure to produce children turned the most beautiful ugly. Hesitant to get into another legal entanglement, she was living with a new man. And Jesus unabashedly had a lengthy and public conversation with her, thereby conferring on her dignity and honor.

> MORE BAD HABITS
>
> **Twelve times he chose duh-sciples to be his inner circle. Now that's a bad habit.**
>
> **TERI HYRKAS**

No wonder she dropped her water jar, ran back to her village, and told everyone, "Come, see a man who told me everything I ever did. Could this be the Messiah?"[4]

Not only did Jesus hang with bad people, but he ate with them, healed them, and restored them to the community. Today, we would still be appalled by Jesus' insistence on talking to, hanging out with, and touching some of the kinds of people we deem outcasts in our societies. Jesus was inclusive, but while he accepted people as they were, he didn't *affirm* them as they were; he transfigured them into the singular images of God they were created to be.

Jesus was born surrounded by animals and died surrounded by criminals. Are animals and outcasts missing from our stories? Jesus spent his life in the company of bad people, and he died as he lived. But like those two thieves on the cross, you can be in the very presence of Jesus and not receive his love. If Jesus had a soft spot in his heart for the waverers, the wanderers, the waywards, and all wayfarers, why don't we? Some will rally and respond to our reaching out, and some will rail on us and reject us. On the cross, Jesus got only 50 percent. How much better do you think you are?

At the same time Jesus was on the cross, showing with his body how much God loves the whole world, he was also reaching out to the two particular people he loved the most—his mother and John. To love the whole world, Jesus became quite tribal and cliquish. He had thousands of members in his fan club and 120 followers with whom he traveled and was pretty tight. He asked 12 to be in his team, invited only 3 into the boardroom, and had only one best friend. The particular becomes universal, the specific general, the concrete cosmic. "Catholicity" means universality out of particularity.[5] Jesus did not love the whole world so much that he loved no one in particular very much. He loved both the glorious whole and the inglorious, vainglorious parts. Even the bad parts.

MORE BAD HABITS

Jesus surrounded himself with theological nitwits who had no or nearly no theological training.

ALLEN GRIFFIN

When Christ takes over, he doesn't efface our personality or deface our facets but sanctifies our uniqueness and purposes it for God's glory. He can use impetuous Peters, humble Andrews, stormy Jameses (like the son of Zebedee), slow Philips, tell-it-like-it-is Bartholomews, gloomy Thomases, calculating Matthews, diminutive Jameses (like the son of Alphaeus), even-keeled Thaddaeuses, passionate Simons, calm Barnabases, confident John Calvins, levelheaded Philipp Melanchthons, and up-and-down Martin Luthers—and you and me.

What makes you flinch? *Gulliver's Travels* author Jonathan Swift (1667–1745) refused to hire any new servant who flinched when told they would be expected to clean other servants' shoes. The "flinch test"—do you flinch when washing the feet of bad or strange people?—is not a bad litmus test for all followers of Jesus.

Jesus has a soft spot for the dechurched and unchurched.

His first visitors, his earliest witnesses, were the strangest of strangers—the lowest of Jews (non-Temple-going shepherds) and the highest of Gentiles (Zoroastrian priests). Jesus is a maestro at making the strange familiar and the familiar strange and calls us to host strangers and the strange in our lives so as not to be estranged from God, each other, and ourselves.

We are also called to follow some we don't think are worthy of God's anointing. Fame, fortune, and education are three of the least accurate measures of divine favor. For Jesus, neither success nor survival is the raison d'être or the summum bonum of human existence. There is, in fact, the Jesus Paradox—that to lose one's life is to gain it.

One time God had to conduct an intervention with Moses because he was so overworked and overwrought. Moses selected seventy people to share the burden of his office. But God also worked beyond this, and the Spirit rested on those that Moses *didn't* believe were called to help lead and hadn't been "ordained."[6]

God mourns over the wanderers, Hosea insisted,[7] and God is married to the backslider, Jeremiah reminded the wandering Israelites.[8] In fact, the best promises in the Bible are reserved for those who have wandered but return to the Lord—the prodigals, the backsliders, the lapsed, the rebels. It is one thing to love the Jesus of the past. It is quite another to love the Jesus of the present—in the outcast, the stigmatized, the unfriended, the exiled, the labeled, the imprisoned, the persecuted, the unlikable. In a world full of many religions, to live a Jesus life is to be interreligious—able to live amicably with and love people of many and of no religions.

An aged Appalachian woman who lived all her life in the high hills and hollers of West Virginia taught her city grand-daughter this formula for a good life:

Wash what is dirty.
Water what is dry.
Heal what is wounded.
Warm what is cold.
Guide what goes off the road.
Love people who are least lovable,
because they need love the most.

Followers of Jesus are loving people, people in love, reaching out to people in pain, often painful people. Globalization makes bad people our neighbors. But in the Pater Noster, the "Our Father," Jesus makes bad people our brothers and sisters.

I collect rubbish art and junk-glass lighting. This is folk art made from throwaways and discarded shards of glass, wood, metal, and concrete. "Nothing can be so ugly that it would be impossible to make something good out of it" is the motto found on the back of the 1945 Berlin Rubbish and Ruins Paintings.

One example of rubbish art is found in the US Holocaust Memorial Museum. It's called "butterfly art." Each butterfly is on a nine-inch square of plywood. The information on a typed sheet of paper glued to the back of each piece explains that it was made out of the rubble of Berlin. Bits of brick, glass, and other building materials have been fastened (I don't think by glue) to the surface of the plywood. The text painted or printed on the front of each piece of plywood says, "In memory of summer 1945" in the upper corners, and beneath each butterfly is the "signature" on these paintings of butterflies, swallows, and flowers: "Made of the rubbish of the ruins of BERLIN."

> **MORE BAD HABITS** 💬
>
> **Picked "favorites" and wasn't bashful about it (John, Peter, James).**
>
> JAKE A. SMITH

Members of the Third Armored (Spearhead) Division in World War II either bought or were given these butterflies and brought them back to the States. Typed on a piece of paper glued to the back of the plywood are these words:

> When the battle of Berlin was over, they met again, just a small group of friends: some painters and designers, and a woman well acquainted with all kinds of fancy-work. They looked around and none of them said a word. What should they say, what did they feel facing the dead under blooming lilacs and the smouldering ruins of their beloved town? With the churches burnt out and their old windows beautifully coloured gone to pieces, the bridges fallen down into the river, the rails bent and the trees burst,

and with mountains of rubbish barring the streets once full of life. What should they do looking at a chaos like this that seemed to have put an end at last to a long but wrong way? Life must go on. It broke the silence. One of them said, they ought to make something of the rubbish that was left. But what?

During summer 1945 in Berlin, butterflies were made piece after piece by the clever and patient hands of men and women who had no paints and brushes to work with and no canvas or paper to work on but who were ready to do almost everything. The light blue color of one butterfly was made from the tiles of a fine delicatessen on Potsdamer Platz and the red brown from the bricks of an old building of Wilhelmstrasse. These butterflies do not look like precious works of art. But those who made them believed that nothing was so ugly that something good and true and beautiful could not be made out of them.

We are all rubbish art.

JESUS SPENT TOO MUCH TIME WITH CHILDREN

CHAPTER TEN

The child in the womb of Elizabeth, leapt with joy. He was,
that little unborn child was, the first messenger of peace. He
recognized the Prince of Peace, he recognized that Christ has
come to bring the good news for you and for me.

MOTHER TERESA, ACCEPTING THE NOBEL PEACE PRIZE IN 1979

JESUS HAD A BAD HABIT of hanging out with children and
even putting children first. "The children get fed first," Jesus
insisted. "Let the little children come," Jesus said.[1]

One of the most memorable moments of my life is the
first time my friend Reggie McNeal and his wife, Cathy,
came to Orcas Island for a visit. Within the first hour they
were there, my home changed. All three of my kids loved to
be in Reggie's presence, and a new spirit of wit and vitality

charged the air we breathed. I learned more about Reggie in that first hour than in all the bestselling books and articles he had written and all the sermons and lectures I had heard him give. My kids knew in that first hour that here was a person you could trust; here was a person who was fun to be around; here was a person who delighted in life and delighted in you.

When Reggie walked into a room, you wanted to be in that room. It must have been that way for children when they were in the presence of Jesus. And it would have been a surprise—to the children *and* to the adults!

Kids in Jesus' day were to be seen and not heard. Small children (under age five) were associated with death. All children were associated with dirt, noise, and annoying habits. It went without saying that they shouldn't bother the rabbi.

Even Jesus' disciples thought he wouldn't want to be interrupted by rambunctious children. Sound familiar? Many of our churches today banish children to distant parts of the building during worship, then bemoan their absence from church when these same kids reach adulthood. Instead of Jesus' "Let the children come unto me," the church says, "Let us babysit your kids while we dazzle you adults in worship."

Jesus' idea of children and childhood was radically different from what was normal in his day. Jesus taught a faith that you might call adultproof. Today we childproof our medicine and our faith, making them as hard for children to get into as possible. In contrast, Jesus made faith child friendly and adult averse, meaning Jesus did everything he could to protect children's faith from adults and to help even the most adultish among us become more childlike so as to get into the Kingdom without messing it up.[2]

Truth is truth whether spoken by a child or a king. There is no halfway Holy Spirit.[3] The question for Jesus was not "How old are you?" but "Do you have ears that hear?" One of the most aberrant features of the gospel story is the tender spot displayed by the wifeless and childless Jesus for children—so tender as to be a hair trigger for Jesus' anger. Any belittling of children prompted an instant emotional storm in Jesus' psyche.

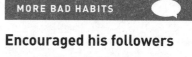

MORE BAD HABITS

Encouraged his followers to take little kids' lunch.

BARRY D. CRAM

The original ending of Hans Christian Andersen's "The Emperor's New Clothes" satirized not the vanity of the high and mighty for keeping a fiction going but mocked the groupthink of the crowd that ended up attacking the child who told the truth—"But he has no robes on at all!"—with sticks and canes.[4] In a world where the emperors of religion and state wear no clothes, and their ministers and minions keep up the pretense, Jesus gave us the child-in-the-crowd's cry of "He's wearing nothing." But Jesus went beyond the warning cry and gave us new clothes to wear. He was a master tailor who modeled the "seamless" clothing of righteousness he customized for real-world, rubber-hits-the-road ministry and mission.

If you want to make Jesus angry, then hamper or hinder or mock a child. Why was Jesus' sensitivity to children so heightened, which was so strikingly out of sync with the dominant cultural norms of his day? Maybe Jesus was stalked by the night-marish specter of the Massacre of the Innocents that attended his birth. The Prince of Peace entered this world only to prompt the piercing cries of innocent children being slaughtered. It was a sound track his soul surely could never mute.

If Jesus was haunted by the reality that his birth caused the death of children, his reaction to children was almost the opposite of his peers. For Jesus, the sight of children inspired protective impulses. For everyone else, children were as much symbols of death as of life. When a child is born today, we immediately feel a collective responsibility. But in Jesus' day, you didn't get too attached to a newborn infant because of the likelihood that they would be ripped from your heart. Almost one out of three children died before their first birthday in the first century.[5] But rather than "fragility motivates distance," for Jesus, fragility obliged responsibility.

In fact, fragility in whatever form elicited in Jesus a sense of responsibility. When Jesus picked up one child and put the child into his lap, he showed his disciples what life and faith in God was truly about, a faith that doesn't look to death but that revels in life. And he showed them that to be responsible in God's sight is to care for the fragile, to care for the children. For within a fragile body is often revealed a bulwark of faith. Jesus touched fragile people, dead people, and "walking dead" people, whether children or adults. But the innocent souls of children, he seemed to say, were closest to the angels, closest to the Kingdom of God.

Jesus treated children as if their relationship with God

was as important as any adult relationship. Jesus constantly sacrificed his rabbinic dignity to reduce the distance between himself and a child.[6] Jesus preached to the children, hoping the adults would get it. That's one reason he told stories.

Stories build identity. And a child's identity is clay in the Potter's hands. Children are made of trust and innocence, an identity constructed out of starlight and moondust—out of the roles and plots and pieces of storybook characters. Children trust a story instinctively and have faith in its beginning and ending. They can make leaps of faith when challenged and know the truth when they hear it.[7] But when your only storybooks are ads and brands and celebrities, and your only narrative compass for identity formation comes from something you built on your own from scratch, your identity will waver at best.

We know that children made up approximately one third of the population in Jesus' day. And it's likely, given the ease with which Jesus pulled a child to his lap from the crowd, that many children came to hear him along with their parents and other adults. And while the adults may have struggled with some of Jesus' stories, it's likely their young charges knew exactly what he meant. They may be fragile, but they are astute. And Jesus' message of God's love and grace, a God who loved *them*, must have been honey to their hearing.

I once heard humorist Anita Renfroe ask parents to remember what it was like to check on your sleeping children to make sure they were still alive. You see them in the crib. They have done nothing for you, given you nothing but sleepless nights and endless days. They have slobbered on you, cried on you, pooped on you, vomited on you. Every bodily fluid that is in them has been dumped on you during the day.

But at night, when they are silent, after giving them every-thing that is in you, you still worry about them. They are so fragile, so vulnerable, the tissue of life so thin. Are they still breathing? You go to their crib and put your hand in the hollow of their back, and you wait for their heartbeat. When you feel that beat, you bask and bathe in the pleasure of their presence. "His little heart is beating!" "She is alive!" That is enough for you. That patting of the hollow of their back and pulse of their heart makes it all worthwhile.

> **MORE BAD HABITS** 💬
>
> **Treated people like children and children like people.**
>
> **DARRIN VICK**

That is the way God is with us. Every day. God relishes your presence. No matter how much trouble you have been or how much distress you have caused, God delights in you just because you are God's child. At least, that's the God Jesus portrayed in his stories and teaching. How the children must have smiled.

For some, Jesus' bad habit was bad to the bone. Celebrity British philosopher C. E. M. Joad believed that Jesus' lion-izing of children defanged the Lion of the tribe of Judah:

It is the anti-intellectual bias of Jesus that I personally found most disquieting. He abuses men of learning, denounces the critical attitude in order to throw into favourable relief that of unquestioning acceptance, and tells people that it is only if they become as little children, and, therefore, as innocent and, presumably, as ignorant as little children, that they can hope to understand Him and be saved.[8]

When the Twelve debate who is the greatest, Jesus does an intervention. But note to what he takes exception. It is not their aspirations to greatness. He doesn't rebuke them for wanting to be great, to be the best. Rather, he rebukes them for their identification of what is the best and the greatest. That's when he takes a little child in his arms and says that this is the "greatest" in the Kingdom.[9] If you aspire to be the best, to true greatness, then make yourself small, little, of no consequence, humble.

Jesus was formed with a womb sound track of humility. The lullaby Mary sang to Jesus while she was pregnant was a praise song, "The Magnificat": "My soul magnifies the Lord. . . . He has brought down the mighty from their thrones and exalted those of humble estate."[10] In the Greek world, humility was not a virtue but a weakness, even a despised quality of life. The noun *humility* does not occur in Greek or Roman writers before the Christian era. The adjective *humble* is common but almost always means mean-spirited, low, groveling, or poor.

Humility, what the ancient world deemed a bone of contention, was a point of connection for Jesus with others. Can

119

you imagine how hard it must have been for Jesus and then Paul to convince people that humility was a positive virtue for a person who was free in Christ? That's why Jesus used a child—not a scholar, soldier, priest, or prophet—to showcase what it meant to be a great follower who returns over and over again to the initial call "Come, follow me!"

And kids do keep us humble. At a time in Arthur Rubinstein's life when his children were still young, this piano virtuoso—one of the greatest pianists of his time and arguably the greatest Chopin interpreter of all time—often had to be away from his family for extended concert tours. Always, when he returned, there was a kind of family celebration. Once, after being away for weeks, as he walked through the door, his little daughter Eva ran up to him, saying, "Daddy, Daddy, you're home. Play for me. Play for me." Rubinstein was delighted. He had been longing to get back to the family, and he sat down at the piano, determined to play as he had never played before. But as he began to play some Chopin, little Eva cried out, "No, Daddy, not the piano, the phonograph!"

The humility of a child for Jesus is not putting yourself down. Humility is accepting the great gifts and talents God has given you but receiving them as *gifts*. These are gifts to be cultivated and invested, not ignored or hoarded. To reject or neglect the gift is to reject or neglect the Giver. We slide into hell on our butts. We soar into heaven on our tiptoes.

A hospital that has caught this bad habit of Jesus is Evelina London Children's Hospital, the first London children's hospital that's been built in a century. A giant atrium in the middle

Your soul may more truly survive in your child's youth
than in your own decrepitude.
GEORGE SANTAYANA

requires periodic window cleaning. But the contract with the company doing the cleaning boasts an interesting codicil: the window cleaners are required to dress up as superheroes. "The children in bed—many with grave illnesses—delight in seeing Superman and Spiderman dangling just inches away from them, on the outside of the glass." It's one of the best parts of the week for both the children and the cleaners.[11]

Someone once wanted to introduce me as one who teaches at universities on both coasts. But while trying to say I was bicoastal (I think), the speaker announced that I was bipolar. I think there is something fundamentally bipolar (not binary) about being a disciple of Jesus (Lion/Lamb, sinner/saint, transcendent/immanent), and the older I get, the more bipolar I become, the more I am going in two opposite directions at the same time. My theology is getting more complex, and my faith is getting more simple. I put them together into one word: simplexity. To follow Jesus is simplex discipleship. Theology conveys thoughts about Christ. Faith conveys Christ. That's simplex discipleship.

The old adage "You are only young once, but you can be immature indefinitely" is not a bad paraphrase of Paul's famous "Grow Up!" passage:

Then we will no longer be infants, tossed back and forth by the waves, and blown here and there by every wind of teaching and by the cunning and craftiness of people in their deceitful scheming. Instead, speaking the truth in love, we will grow to become in every respect the mature body of him who is the head, that is, Christ.[12]

Simplex discipleship means we are to grow up (become more mature and adult) and grow down (become more like children) at the same time. Kidults refuse to grow up and mature. Adulkids refuse to leave their childhoods as they mature into adulthood. Adulkids grow into their childhoods. Some of your best moments as an adult are when you act most like a child, and some of your best memories as an adult are of your childhood. Pablo Picasso believed that it took him six or seven decades to become young.

The church has seen children as a separate species requiring special programming and differentiated approaches. But those who reach the imagination of children best—children's authors—deny that children are a separate species. "I don't write for children," Maurice Sendak said in his final video interview. "I write—and somebody says, 'That's for children!'"[13]

> **MORE BAD HABITS** 💬
>
> **He trusted in divine Providence. He didn't plan ahead on the day that he fed the 5,000.**
>
> MARY WISNER MILLER

Seven decades earlier J. R. R. Tolkien denied there was any such thing as writing for children. More recent children's authors like Neil Gaiman have echoed the same sentiments. But perhaps the greatest and most ardent advocate for this notion was C. S. Lewis.

Lewis attacked any attempt to treat adulthood as superior to childhood, a sort of existential upgrade, using childishness as a put-down and seeing immaturity as a negative quality:

> Critics who treat *adult* as a term of approval, instead of as a merely descriptive term, cannot be adult themselves. To be concerned about being grown up, to admire the grown up because it is grown up, to blush at the suspicion of being childish; these things are the marks of childhood and adolescence. And in childhood and adolescence they are, in moderation, healthy symptoms. Young things ought to want to grow. But to carry on into middle life or even into early manhood this concern about being adult is a mark of really arrested development. When I was ten, I read fairy tales in secret and would have been ashamed if I had been found doing so. Now that I am fifty I read them openly. When I became a man I put away childish things, including the fear of childishness and the desire to be very grown up.[14]

Lewis banners this as a marker of how we evaluate our creative and intellectual growth over the course of life. The ultimate in "arrested development," Lewis writes, is not in losing childhood tastes but "in failing to add new things. . . . I now enjoy Tolstoy and Jane Austen and Trollope as well as fairy tales and I call that growth: if I had had to lose the fairy tales in order to acquire the novelists, I would not say that I had grown but only that I had changed."[15]

For followers of Jesus, aging should also be younging. It's the rare child who makes it to adulthood without having some version of the "don't be a child" syndrome drilled into him or her. But for Jesus, when a child of God grows up, the child inside remains, as long as God's fullness is released and a mature faith is grown. The Jesuits have a saying: "*Deus semper major*," or "God ever greater." In an adultlike faith, ego gets bigger as God gets smaller. In a childlike faith, God gets bigger as ego gets smaller.

This bad habit of Jesus makes us more adult in our theology and more childlike (not childish) in our faith. After all, Jesus said, "There will be no grownups in heaven."[16] Or more precisely, "Unless you change and become like little children, you will never enter the kingdom of heaven."[17]

Jesus' bad habit of paying attention to children needs to be our bad habit too. Children must be at the heart of the church if it's to be a Jesus church. And the child must always be in our hearts if we are to be true Jesus followers.

The same God who says, "I will carry you; and I will bear you and I will deliver you";[18] the same God who promises to be our "dwelling place, and underneath are the everlasting arms";[19] the same God who "took the children in his arms":[20]

that very same God became a child who let us pick him up and risked letting us hold him in our arms.

And look how we held in our arms the precious Son of God. We beat him and we pierced him and we crucified him. And how did God respond to our treatment of God's child? That same God's arms opened wide on the cross and signed "I love you" with his very life.

JESUS EITHER TALKED TOO MUCH OR WAS SILENT WHEN HE SHOULD HAVE TALKED

CHAPTER ELEVEN

JESUS IS EASY TO TALK TO. Then—and now.[1] He does have the bad habit of speaking his mind and not trying to please people.

But Jesus seemed either to be talking when he should have been silent or silent when he should have been talking. When his life depended on him saying nothing, he said something. When his life depended on him saying something, he said nothing. Jesus had a bad habit of mouthing off and shutting up at exactly the wrong moments. But Jesus loved to listen.

In the presence of spies, plants, haters, and other forms of ecclesiastical espionage, Jesus said things he knew would get him in trouble. In fact, Jesus was fearless in talking. Even when Jesus saw the haters in his midst, he gave the religious leaders exactly what they needed to prosecute him for blasphemy.[2] Far from the *Deus absconditus* (hidden God) people usually think of, Jesus was the *Deus loquacious* (talking God). Everywhere he went, he was talking and teaching, discussing and debating. Who said to be deep meant to be silent?

But then when his life depended on him defending himself in front of Pilate, Jesus remained silent and "made no reply."[3] There comes a time when nothing more can be said. For Jesus, silence was a form of speech, rejecting a normal flow of words with the meaning of the unsaid. As Job would say, "How can I reply to you? I put my hand over my mouth."[4] Besides, an empty tomb speaks louder than words.

Herod couldn't down him.

Satan couldn't detour him.

Hatred couldn't discourage him.

Adulation couldn't deter him.

Death couldn't destroy him.

The grave couldn't detain him.

The ultimate in eloquence is the abstention of all eloquence. Or as Meister Eckhart put it in the fourteenth century, "If you think you know something about God and describe it in words, the God you have described is not God. God is greater than your terminology. God is far greater than your language. [God] is inexpressible."[5]

To express the inexpressible, there is a time for silence and a time for speech. Just as the Israelites were led by cloud and fire, so the mystery we call God leads us through life by the cloud of humble unknowing and the fire of confident knowing. The unsearchable riches of Christ demand awed silence as well as trumpet blare. For Jesus prayer time with his Father was as much a listening post and watchtower as it was a talkfest or question-and-answer time.

Jesus talked in gestures, which frustrated his disciples especially. Rather than explain what it means to "remember him," for example, he did four things with bread, as Augustine was one of the first to notice: offering, thanking, breaking, sharing. When anyone asked, "What do you mean by that?" he would take it, offer it up, bless it and give thanks for it, break it, and share it. "Jesus, what does that mean?" and once again he would take the bread, offer it up . . . The church is the body of Christ, the ongoing incarnation of God's grace and love. The church is to be an offering. In that offering is freedom. The church is to be a blessing. In that blessing is expressed gratitude. The church is to be broken. In that breaking there is obedience. The church is to be shared. In that giving of itself there is love.

The word mystery is bandied about recklessly. If a mystic is one who continually covets and cultivates the presence of God and the fullness of truth, then Jesus was a mystic. For Jesus, the life of faith is one of "living the mystery." In fact, the church is dying for its need to nail everything down and its failure to let the mystery shine. In making God "reasonable," the Enlightenment effectively banished mystery, since a rational God is by definition not a mysterious one. The divine mystery is a mystery that will never be "solved" like in a detective novel.

But just as we mourn not as those who have no hope,[6] we revel in mystery not as the world understands mystery. To live the mystery is not to live as if life were inexplicable or unexplainable but to live knowing that we see life "through a glass, darkly." No matter how much Windex and scholarly elbow grease we apply, our knowledge is inherently limited. Since we are created in God's image, we are capable of knowing truth. Reality is reasonable, and one day we will know as we are known.[7] Because of Jesus, God is the Known Unknown. One day the mystery will be made manifest, and the secret will be no longer hidden.

But until then, the closer and deeper we inhabit the abundant life, the more the mystery shines with a deepening sheen. There is more to light than meets the eye. How much more there is to the Light of the World than the eye can take in! How much more there is to the Vine than the tongue can taste or tell!

Jesus refused to get entangled in words. He often preferred silence to words. There comes a time for anyone who has something to say to step forward and be silent. In the face of a woman caught in adultery, Jesus deemed silence the best response. There is sometimes great power in silence. Jesus fought fire not with fiery words but with a cloud of dust from his silent writing on the ground. God's trumpet sounds for the widows who have put their lives on the line silently, who have given all they have—not for those who blow their own horns with noisy offerings.

The church started having a problem with silence very early in its history. In the fifth century, the church excommunicated all of the mimes in its midst.

Not all silence is reverential or right or silent. Sometimes silence can be revolutionary and noisy.

Sometimes silence can be cowardice. The serpent addresses both Adam and Eve, but Adam lets Eve do the talking.

Sometimes silence can be a lie. There is a saying in Africa, one that applies powerfully to the problem of abuse: silence is the biggest lie we tell.

Sometimes silence is healing and helps the pain go away. In the most recent research on posttraumatic stress disorder, those who heal the fastest are those who keep moving forward without going backward and digging up words and thoughts of the horrors of the past, proving true an old English saying: "Least said, soonest mended." When physical exhaustion overtakes the body, sleep is the remedy. When spiritual exhaustion overtakes the body, silence is the remedy.

> **MORE BAD HABITS** 💬
>
> **He kept silent instead of witnessing when someone asked what truth is.**
>
> **DAVID SCAFIDE**

Jesus had a bad habit of never writing anything down. You can just hear one or more of his disciples saying, "Jesus, write it down!" Jesus *could* write.[8] So why did he avoid writing? Why did he not put his teachings and feelings down in stone, only in sand (once)?[9]

Did he fear the idolatry of words? Did he want us to realize that his ultimate teaching (and ours) is in flesh and blood, not in parchment and papyrus? Did he not want us to do what the Pharisees and scribes had done with the written word? The heart of Jesus' ministry was not what he said to be inscribed on lambskin or limestone but what he did: he died on the cross, rose from the dead, and promised to return to establish a new heaven and new earth.

> **MORE BAD HABITS**
>
> **He can be bossy. He doesn't always answer me when I want Him to, and seems slow to show up. He doesn't make life the way I want it. . . . And He just won't leave me alone.**
>
> **CONNIE BELL PRICE**

When a letter was sent in the first century, the messenger who brought the letter was almost as important as the message. Jesus is the Message *and* the Messenger. We, his disciples, are his letters. As Paul says, "I bear on my body the marks of Jesus."[10] This is the highest level of autograph, for one's being to be the parchment for the autograph of Jesus and the stylus of the Spirit. For his words to be written on hearts is the prophesied New Covenant of Jeremiah.[11]

This is not to say that the early Christians weren't writers. Early Christian communities were cottage industries of textuality, collecting, editing, commenting on, producing, and circulating codices of various books and letters and other writings. "The followers of Jesus would trace their way in writing."[12]

But certain parts of Jesus' teaching were so sacred that they were never written down, only committed to oral transmission. If Jesus had stayed, that which was in him would have remained in him. Because Jesus went away, but not before giving us the Holy Spirit, that which was in him is now in us.

JESUS BROKE THE RULES

CHAPTER TWELVE

FROM HEALING ON THE SABBATH, to eating with unwashed hands and unclean people, to allowing his disciples to swipe food from another person's field, to declaring himself God, Jesus flouted rules, violated taboos, and promoted behavior nightmarishly wrong in the eyes of the establishment. Jesus would break the rules to bless you.

Jesus wasn't just terrible at keeping the Sabbath; in the eyes of the religious establishment, he sinned against the God of the Sabbath. A Jesus world was a world turned upside down, as frightening to the powers that be as nuclear fission and fallout. No wonder the authorities began to track every move he made.

Jesus broke not only religious rules but also cultural rules. Jesus would have scandalized his town by not being married. You had a duty to your ancestors and your family to marry and reproduce. Later rabbis said, "Seven things are condemned in heaven, and the first of these is a man without a woman."

Jesus didn't break rules just to be a rebel. Jesus had something even greater to show us and tell us every time he pushed the envelope. For example, Jesus revolutionized Sabbath keeping with three affirmations:

1. Sabbath is made for humans, not humans for Sabbath.[1]
2. Jesus is Lord of the Sabbath.[2]
3. It is lawful to do good on the Sabbath.[3]

Jesus had an overriding, wild-card rule: break any of the rules of the Sabbath sooner than do anything outright unkind or unloving or unsupportive of life. Always support life. To support death, not life, may be the ultimate sin against the Holy Ghost. He didn't so much reject the law as revision it the way God intended it whenever its interpretation by the institution did harm to people. What mattered to Jesus was not keeping the law but helping hurting people. Everything else was relative to that, including Jesus' freedom to break the law when it was breaking the backs and spirits of people.[4]

Not only did Jesus' frequent breaks with tradition reveal a lesson, but they pointed to the truth of who Jesus is—the Son of God, who creates the rules in the first place. Who to know God's intent better than Jesus?

If I want to play chess, I must obey the rules. If I don't play, the rules have no authority over me. Since Jesus opted out of playing the religion game of the Temple elite, the rules of the game had no authority over him. But the cost of opting out was his life.

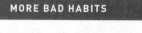

MORE BAD HABITS

Never voted. Never went to church. Never "settled down" and had a family.

BOB HOSTETLER

Some people are held together by rules. To be held by Jesus is to be held together by a relationship with God. No rules save Jesus. If Jesus rules your life, the Jesus Rule will cover every situation: Rules or Right?

God doesn't play by the rules, at least not our rules. God *sets* the rules. Humans love rules. Hence *Robert's Rules of Order*, which rules the church. We are addicted to the fruit of the tree of the knowledge of rules. God is love and life. God rules by who God is—Love and Life.

The Greek Orthodox Church reminds us of this in its many images of Christ Pantocrator, "Ruler of All." The church will always sink deeper and deeper into a morass of inertia, desuetude, and despair when it forgets the key word that opens all doors and frees all souls: Jesus Christ Pantocrator. You don't have to love Jesus to be enthralled by life, but life is immensely enriched and enchanted the more you know Jesus.

The Hebrew word for "know" is *yada*, a relational word of great intimacy. This word doesn't mean to know *about* something but to be in intimate relationship with something or someone. To know Jesus is to be in relationship with Jesus. You can know *about* Jesus' life and times. But that's not the same as *knowing* Jesus firsthand and face-to-face. God cares less about what we know than about how we love and whom we love. For God, relationships always trump rules.

The word *economy* has a family connotation. The Greek words *oikos* (home) and *nomos* (law) mean the law of God's household. In God's home, the house rules apply! And the only rule God has is the rule of love. And the rule of love leads to different worship than the red carpet, the White House, or Wall Street.

God does not love in theory but in action. The Creator did not send us a statement in the sky, simply saying, "I love you." God sent a Savior to earth who showed God's love by living with us, dying for us, and rising in us.

The law was written on stone. Love is written on the heart: "I will give you a new heart and put a new spirit in you; I will remove from you your heart of stone and give you a heart of flesh."[5] A stony heart pumps icy legalism through the veins. But a new heart—a heart re-newed by God—pumps pure blood and pure love.

You can't hold your life together with the twine of rules. You can hold your life together only with the relational cords of grace and love.

Jesus' bad habit of rule breaking is a lesson for our own

relationships. To reject someone's idea gets often conveyed as a rejection or condemnation of that person. Can we think someone wrong and still be in right relationship with them? Sometimes a relationship can be sealed simply with a handshake, not a harness or a rule.

Every child needs rules. You "grow up" by learning the rules. But there comes a time when you stop living by the rules and start loving from the heart.

Jesus had a real problem with those who lived only by the rules. In fact, the law keepers were some of the people Jesus had the most conflict with—those who look good on the outside but stink from the inside: "Get this and get it straight. The problem is not what goes into a person from the outside that defiles him, but what comes out of the person from the inside. . . . From inside, from a person's heart, come evil things that make a person unclean."[6] Jesus doesn't want to control us from the outside but to guide and channel us from the inside.

MORE BAD HABITS

Gave bad medical advice. My doctor and other medical professionals would not approve of 40 day fasts.

HOLLY BOARDMAN

Critical and censorious spirits who view their mission in life to be yardsticks and scales run the risk of developing wooden and metallic souls. Those who have been forgiven much will love much, Jesus said.[7] If your church is not loving enough, maybe there is not enough forgiving going on.

Today's churches need to cultivate Jesus' bad habit of breaking some traditions and rules and living in such a way that makes the heart sing and the mind dance. "Why, my soul, are you downcast? Why so disturbed within me? Put your hope in God, for I will yet praise him, my Savior and my God."[8] Don't sink into the arms of despair; sink into the arms of God, which open the artillery of heaven. This bad habit of Jesus gets into our bones the flesh and blood and breath of Jesus until "dem bones" live again and "dem dry bones" dance.

> **MORE BAD HABITS** 💬
>
> **He talked politics and religion . . . usually over dinner.**
>
> **DAVID SCAFIDE**

JESUS ENJOYED THE COMPANY OF WOMEN (NOT JUST MEN)

CHAPTER THIRTEEN

JESUS WAS REVOLUTIONARY for his time in many ways, but nowhere was he more revolutionary than in his relationships with and treatment of women. His actions stunned everyone, even his own disciples.

Jesus shared his life with women; he opened his mind and heart to women; he loved the company of women. His cradling, compassionate touch stunned women used to the careless touch of their culture. And that cradling, compassionate touch got Jesus into a lot of trouble.

A word about the etymology of that word *compassion*. Jesus loved Hosea 6:6: "I desire mercy, not sacrifice." Jesus even said that "if you had known what these words mean, . . . you would not have condemned the innocent."[1] The Hebrew word for "mercy" is *chesed*; the Greek word for mercy is *eleos* (as in *Kyrie eleison*, or "Lord, have mercy"). *Eleos* words are found everywhere in the New Testament, and Jesus chose the word to feature in his Beatitudes: "Blessed are the merciful, for they shall be mercied."[2] Just as God has mercied us, we are to mercy others. No one mercied women more than Jesus.

The Greek *eleos* is related to the word for "compassion," which means "gutted." We get squeamish when we hear a word we love like *compassion* connected both in Hebrew and Greek to words like *entrails* or *guts* or *bowels* or even *womb*, which introduces a maternal quality of God.[3] But perhaps for us it means that Jesus felt for the women in his world so strongly that it resonated in his gut. His gut reaction was to have compassion for them. His heart was in his gut when he saw what they had to go through in the culture in which he lived. In Mark 1:41, Jesus' heart was "gutted" by the leper's plight. In Matthew 20:34, Jesus' heart was "gutted" by the two blind men at Jericho. In Luke 15:20, the father saw his son far off and his "gut" reacted.

But nothing stirred the gut of Jesus more than the plight of women, on whom he bestowed compassion and whom he empowered like no one else in the ancient world. No wonder women were the first to the Resurrection, the foremost among the faithful, and on the front lines of faithfulness. No wonder Jesus featured women as main characters in his own story and in the stories he told.

Already at the beginning of his ministry, Jesus would set a precedent for his feelings about women. As Jesus and his disciples traveled through Samaria, Jesus stopped to speak to a Samaritan woman by historic Jacob's Well. Not only was she a scorned Samaritan and, as a woman, seen as a second-class citizen, but Jesus was alone with her when he spoke with her. When his disciples arrived, they were shocked. How could their teacher risk his reputation with bad habits like this? Wasn't this behavior bad for a proper Jew, let alone their Master Rabbi? Jesus took time to show compassion to the woman, which silenced them and set them straight right away. The disciples followed him to the town, no doubt joining the curious bystanders in pondering whether anyone with bad habits like loosely talking with women could actually be the Messiah.

What was scandalous about the encounter was not just that Jesus spoke to the woman alone but the nature of their conversation. Why does Jesus ask her about her husbands? Because in Jesus' day, women could not exist on their own without a man, either a husband or a relative. Wives were dependent, chattel of their husbands. They could never initiate a divorce, only be at the receiving end. The law (interpreted by the current Pharisees) allowed men to divorce their wives for the pettiest reasons or the most unsubstantiated accusations. Without recourse, women could not only be blamed for their plight but could be passed about from man to man with little hope of a happy life. Or worse, they could be cast onto the street, alone, without sustenance or care.

Jesus' teaching on divorce was meant to prevent women from being pawns in a male-dominated board game.[4]

All of the women in Jesus' life were treated with mutuality and esteem, and this particular Samaritan woman who confessed to five husbands was no exception to the rule. Far from a critique of her "promiscuity," Jesus showed tenderness and compassion for her plight. This woman had been mistreated again and again, tossed around like a toy, jilted by lovers and the law. Jesus saw her as a beloved child of God who had endured much abuse and would gladly hear the words of that coming Messiah for whom she would be more than a tart-with-heart story, but a God's-art-from-God's-heart story.

"He told me my whole life," she would say. Jesus knew not just her life but her heart. And he let her know, as he did all women, that she was made for beauty and truth and goodness too.

> **MORE BAD HABITS**
>
> **Hung out with women, depended upon their financial support, and defended them when they were attacked.**
>
> **J. R. BRIGGS**

Jesus is the first person in recorded history, in fact, to critique the "male gaze," saying that "anyone who looks at a woman lustfully has already committed adultery with her in his heart."[5] Jesus took the proverb "As he thinks in his heart, so is he"[6] seriously but went beyond "Don't do it" to "Don't even *think* about it!"[7] This was not just a moral principle but a social one. Jesus was looking out for the safety and welfare of women—divorcées, widows, and others.

What the mind feeds upon is what the soul feeds upon. Yet Jesus advocated the treatment of adulteresses as adults ripe for forgiveness. Jesus deemed prostitutes not objects, but he esteemed them as subjects worthy of compassion and love. Jesus' call to repent is the call to come home, to return to where you came from.

Like many other women who flourished in Jesus' presence, the woman at the well would megaphone his mission. She would magnify the Messiah's coming to all who would listen. She had been waiting for a Savior all her life. So had others. Samaria was outcast by Jerusalem. But God had not forgotten them. They believed that. Now Jesus confirmed it.

This encounter with the woman at the well set a precedent for many of Jesus' encounters with women. Jesus didn't fear social stigmas or follow the politically correct habits of his day. Most of Jesus' habits were revolutionary in the eyes of his contemporaries and outrageous to the Jerusalem authorities. But Jesus acted according to his heart, not according to their rules.

In the Scriptures, we see numerous encounters Jesus had with women. In addition to the woman at the well, Jesus did not scold the woman who touched his robe as he traveled, but he commended her faith. He did not automatically condemn an adulteress but spoke with her and forgave her sins. He healed a woman with demons, believed to be Mary of Magdala, who then became one of his most trusted disciples.

We know of women who funded Jesus' ministry. There were any number of other women who followed him as a disciple, and even those later such as Junia, the mysterious woman "apostle" of Romans 16.

In fact, when Jesus teaches in the Jerusalem Temple, he does so in the court, in which all are welcome, including women and children. It is here that he commends the poor widow who puts her last coin into the Temple jar. In all of these cases, Jesus does not scold these women for touching him or speaking to him. But he has compassion on all of them.

In Jesus' day, to say women were second-class citizens would be a kindness. Women were to keep out of sight and not approach a rabbi. In fact, it was a sin to teach a woman the Torah. Women were simply not worthy to learn such high and holy things. Yet Jesus saw all women as worthy, even young female children, what we would today call "adolescent girls." Imagine the pious outrage when Jesus touched an adolescent girl, a hemorrhaging woman, a Gentile female, and a woman he healed of demons.[8] All of these were deemed unclean. It was bad enough that Jesus touched men to heal them. But to touch *women*!

He healed the adolescent daughter of Jairus, touching her hand, just as he healed the son of the widow at Nain. He healed a crippled woman, whom he called a "daughter of Abraham." He healed the child of a Syrophoenician woman. And he commended them for their great faith.[9]

One of Jesus' first acts was to heal the mother-in-law of

Simon Peter, at which she rose and began to serve them food. Allowing her to serve him would also have been not just odd but at odds for any self-respecting rabbi. This oddness would become a bad habit for Jesus, as he spent countless hours at Lazarus's home in Bethany in the company of Mary and Martha.

Jesus obviously had a close relationship with Lazarus's sisters Mary and Martha. He loved Martha's cooking, and he loved the attention Mary lavished on him. Her pouring of expensive perfumed oil over his head angered Jesus' disciples and may have been the straw that broke the camel's back in Judas's mind, causing him to betray his Master Rabbi. Whether the woman who poured oil onto Jesus' feet and wiped it with her hair was an earlier occurrence or whether a revised telling of Mary's story, we cannot know. But it's clear that Jesus had no problem having women speak with him, touch him, travel with him, fund him, cook for him, and follow him as disciples.

In fact, the respect Jesus accords for women is simply unprecedented in the ancient world. The stories in Scripture of Mary and Martha not only include the women but put the women in the forefront, over his friend Lazarus! The focus of the stories is the women. When Lazarus falls ill, the women send for Jesus, and it is to them that he comes and hears their anger, their doubts, their pleading, their tears. And it is for them that he raises his friend from the dead.

Each and every time Jesus heals someone, and in this case raises the dead, it is to point to his identity as the Messiah and to point to God's power and glory in the here and now. Whether Jairus's daughter or Lazarus, Jesus takes his time getting to the scene of their deaths. He doesn't rush. In fact, he appears to purposely dawdle so that he not just heals them but resurrects them. One could say that these are deliberate signs to show God's resurrection power for all God's people. But in every case of resurrection, women are intimately involved in the story.

In the case of Jairus's daughter, Jesus is slowed down by the hemorrhaging woman, whom he stops to speak to after she touches his robe. The story of the hemorrhaging woman is deliberately inserted within the story of Jairus's daughter so as to show the meaning of faith and the power of God. But once again, it is a woman who demonstrates that depth of faith! She is the "teaching insert."

In the case of Lazarus, Mary and Martha show the meaning of faith as well, indicating that they know if Jesus had come, Lazarus would have been saved from death. Jesus then is free to show that earthly time and place have no meaning in God's time and place. God's power is not stunted or stopped by death. On the contrary, the conversation Jesus has with the women allows for the awesome act of God that raises Lazarus still wearing his burial garments.

Women in particular witnessing Jesus' miracles is nothing new. Although Jesus appears to have had a strained relationship with his family throughout the Scriptures, he always maintains the closest relationship with his mother. He helps his mother in his inaugural miracle—changing water into wine for the wedding feast in Cana. It's obvious that this is a family affair and that Mary believes in who Jesus is (see chapter 3). She knows he is capable of performing miracles. Perhaps she isn't sure how he will do it. But she knows he can. Jesus seems at first to dislike using God's power to fulfill something that seems as petty as providing drink for the already sodden partygoers. But he honors his mother and creates from that simple task a meaningful, metaphor-rich demonstration of who he is and God's messianic plan for the final Kingdom feast.

This initial miracle sets the tone for Jesus' entire ministry, and Jesus' last parables return to the metaphor of the feast, with the connotation that all will be bountifully fed and watered. We can't be sure whether Mary doubted her son during the course of his ministry. We know she was worried when he began to forgive sins and push the envelope with the Pharisees. We know she felt disgraced when he read in the synagogue in Nazareth and declared himself their Savior but denied miracles to his hometown. But still, it is Mary who waits by the cross through the wretched moments of Jesus' death, along with Mary Magdalene and Mary wife of Clopas. Even at the cross, Jesus takes pain to take care of his

> **MORE BAD HABITS**
>
> **Jesus had the awful habit of talking to women as if they were not only human but *gasp* peers!**
>
> **JEN CLARK TINKER**

mother, as well as forging a bond between her and his new family of disciples. Mary goes on to be part of the ministry team Jesus leaves behind, and the rest of his family joins her, no doubt in large measure because of Mary's urging. Even in his death, Jesus honors and respects women.

The first people to see Jesus after the Resurrection are women. He speaks first to Mary Magdalene at the tomb. He tells her to report to the disciples in a time when a woman's testimony would have been worthless. Jesus forces his disciples to think differently about women. We know that later some of his disciples have great problems doing this. But we also know Jesus challenges that thinking in them, most of all by giving the most important message of all—that of his resurrection—first to Mary, his beloved disciple. In fact, Mary enjoys the official title in the Roman Catholic Church of "apostle to the apostles."

Jesus taught women, breaking the rule of the day that women were not to be taught the sacred texts. Yet Jesus wrote them into nearly every story. He taught them, he healed them, he touched them, he loved them—and they followed him and funded his ministry, women like Joanna and Susanna, who after being healed became benefactors. Even those he didn't touch directly brought their children to hear him.

We do know that Jesus' disciples eventually "got it," because the Scriptures point specifically to Jesus' inclusiveness of women. There is the story of Elizabeth and Mary, a meeting of the two women who would bear the Messiah and his proclaimer. In the story of Elizabeth, it is she who is noted for her great faith, not her husband, who fails in his faith and is silenced for the duration of her pregnancy. In the story of Mary, she accepts God's mission for her immediately and without question while Joseph frets and wonders how to deal with it all. Even at Jesus' presentation at the Temple, Jesus is not just blessed by the priest but also by a prophetess. The story of the prophetess Anna's proclamation about Jesus as a baby foreshadows the inclusiveness that women would experience throughout Jesus' ministry.

Throughout Scripture, women are not just recognized, they are honored as the shining examples of how to have deep, trusting, enduring faith. You could even say that for Jesus, women are metaphors of what faith looks like in the face of hardship and an unjust world.

Jesus draws upon the Hebrew Scriptures in everything he does and says. He knows them inside and out, and uses them pointedly in his storytelling and in his actions. Jesus' inclusion of women has scriptural roots as well as personal ones.

Matthew's genealogy reminds us of five women in Jesus' personal history: Tamar, Rahab, Ruth, Bathsheba, and Mary. In a time when families were recognized by males, it is odd that these women should appear in a genealogy at all, let alone the one indicating the Messiah. Yet these women are highlighted as contributing to the birthright of the Messiah. Each of the women is a key member of Jesus' birth history in the line of David, and all have in some way been compromised by scandal. Each bore in her story of sexual tangles and triangles the messianic promise. And the message of each

Hebrew story regarding these women? Uncompromising loyalty and great faith! Each life becomes an integral story line of the timeline that bears the coming Messiah, a Messiah who will free not just men, but women as well.

As Jesus names the crippled woman "daughter of Abraham," so are all who have great faith sons and daughters of God. God's covenant is with men, women, and all of creation. As Jesus tells the Pharisees time and time again, it's not about your bloodline but about your heartbeat. And the people in Jesus' life with the most beautiful and worshipful hearts were women. The women in Jesus' life show us perhaps best how to live a life of faith. Astonishingly, Jesus himself contrasts the deep faith of women with the shallow faith of others, even the shortcomings of his own disciples.[10] He calls attention to the pure faith of a widow and her mite, a Gentile woman, a woman who touched his robe, and Mary Magdalene, who believed when she heard his voice. The highest compliment Jesus ever paid to anyone, including his closest disciples, he paid to a woman who anointed his body, saying, "Whenever you remember me, remember her."[11]

The very things most celebrated by people who hate Christianity are the very gifts of Christianity itself. Before Christianity, there were cults that practiced all sorts of human sacrifice as well as self-mutilation and self-castration. Before Christianity, the weak were despised, the poor maligned, the handicapped abandoned. Before Christianity, infanticide was rampant, slavery run of the mill, and gladiatorial combat a form of entertainment. In Jesus' day, Corinth was famous for its temple prostitutes,[12] continuing a long-standing tradition symbolized by the Corinthian athlete Xenophon, who won the footrace at the seventy-ninth Olympic Games (464 BCE) and in thanks to the gods presented a hundred slave women to the temple of Aphrodite at Corinth, a "pious act" praised and memorialized for all time by the Greek poet Pindar (522–433 BCE). Aristotle (384–322 BCE) not only condoned institutionalized slavery but provided an elaborate argument in favor of it. As if that weren't enough, Aristotle called man "begotten" and woman "misbegotten," and because a woman's reasoning was "without authority" accepted no female students.[13]

> **MORE BAD HABITS**
>
> **Liked to associate with the unclean: lepers, the poor guy at the tomb, pigs, the woman who bled for 12 years, and he tops it off by holding a dead girl's hand!**
>
> **KELLY CHEWNING**

Only Jesus and his followers known as the church insisted on the concept of human dignity and the value of every human soul. Only the church built hospitals and took care of the abandoned and disabled. Only the church celebrated charity and selflessness as the highest virtue and elevated the status of women. The educator, reformer, and suffragist Frances Willard (1839–1898) pushed the Women's Christian Temperance Union to get behind Prohibition with the motto "Do Everything!" This "do everything" mentality can trace its origins to Jesus' "love everyone" mentality.

To be sure, the church has often lost its way and sold out to the surrounding culture. The church's greatest theologian, Thomas Aquinas (1225–1274), writing in what some say is the greatest theological treatise of all time, *Summa Theologica*, followed in Aristotle's "misbegotten" wake and inserted these words about women: "As regards the individual nature, woman is defective and misbegotten. . . . The production of woman comes from defect in the active force or from some material indisposition, or even from some external influence; such as that of a south wind, which is moist. . . . By such a kind of subjection woman is naturally subject to man, because in man the discretion of reason predominates."[14] Friedrich Nietzsche (1844–1900), who single-handedly shaped the direction of Western philosophy, was only following a long-standing tradition when he jokingly said of women that they were indescribably more evil than men: "Are you visiting women? Do not forget the whip."[15]

It took 1,800 years for the majority of Christian theologians to question seriously the morality of slavery. Some are still fighting over the oppression of women in the church and culture. So it behooves everyone to be a little humble. The first modern Olympic Games in 1896 had no female competitors, and by the Stockholm Olympics in 1912, there were only 48 women out of 2,407 participants. Not until 1975 were Connecticut women legally allowed to take out loans or open bank accounts without their husbands' permission. Women were not admitted to Princeton or Yale before 1969, and not until 1984 did New York state law recognize that a sexual attack on a wife constitutes rape. To this day, how heavily does the thumb rest on the scale when women or minority candidates are considered for positions in the church?

A bent twig snaps back. The long-term consequences of grievous injustice and goaded passivity, of stewing and seething in the pot of history, is something that Florence Nightingale (1820–1910) off-loaded with more than a touch of tetchiness. "The-Lady-with-the-Lamp" warned how "the great reformers of the world turn into the great misanthropists, if circumstances of organisation do not permit them to act. Christ, if he had been a woman, might have been nothing but a great complainer."[16] No one was more sensitive to how oppression can suck the marrow out of a woman's soul than Jesus was.

Another social reformer who all her life battled on against unimaginable odds was Sojourner Truth (1797–1883). Truth spoke for more than herself when she explained the impact this one man, Jesus of Nazareth, had on her life. Sojourner Truth was an escaped slave who became an abolitionist and women's rights activist. During a gathering of preachers and abolitionists in the home of Harriet Beecher Stowe (author of *Uncle Tom's Cabin*), Truth was asked if she preached from the Bible. She answered no, because she could not read. "When I preaches," she said, "I has just one text to preach from, an' I always preaches from this one. My text is, 'When I found Jesus.'"

Women throughout history have shared that same

testimony as Sojourner Truth: freedom and wholeness were found "when I found Jesus." Some people have to travel through a tornado or flood or fire or cancer to discover that self-help salvation is wrong: all our dreams and desires do not already lay in our hands or at our feet. Others, like Sojourner Truth, discover that the Scriptures are right about where salvation comes from: all their dreams and desires lie ready at the feet of Jesus.

JESUS FOCUSED ON THE LITTLE THINGS IN LIFE

CHAPTER FOURTEEN

JESUS HAD A BAD HABIT of fixating on the little and ignoring the big—the big people, the big deals, the big ideas. Jesus did not sidle up to the movers and shakers but sat among the forsaken and the inconsequential, the lame and the left behind. For Jesus, good things come in small packages. Jesus takes the little and weak and lifts them up. Satan takes the large and gifted and brings them down.

Jesus did not mount campaigns against the social structures of his day but focused on the needs of neighbors and individuals. In a culture that said you were of value only if you did big things in big ways to effect big changes with big consequences, Jesus liked the small—small people, small differences, small matters—as a strategy to save the world. "Where two or three are gathered in my name, there am I in the midst of them," Jesus promised.[1] You find God in the midst: the midst of the everyday, the midst of the mundane, the midst of the obvious. An anonymous haiku sounds like something Jesus might have said: "To see small matters/And to see that small matters/Are not small matters."

"Who dares despise the day of small things?" the priest-prophet Zechariah declared.[2] Look around you. In the makes-no-sense economy of grace, God takes your little—pot of oil, two mites, five pebbles, sewing needle, string, jawbone, loaves and fishes—and blesses it into endless greatness. Take your little pot of oil, turn it into a prayer that you place in God's hands, and watch what happens. Put your little into the hands of the one who holds the world in hand and see little become large. Absurdly small differences make colossally big differences. Coca-Cola is 99.8 percent water and sugar. A global empire was created on 0.2 percent. What's your 0.2 percent?

In some ways, Jesus' parable of the mustard seed highlights his bad habit of lionizing the little and the despised. Mustard is an undesirable, insatiable weed, unwanted by any respectable gardener. Jesus uses a toxic weed to describe the covenant but points to the unsuitable nature of the covenant holders as those typically disqualified by the keepers of the law. Jesus' idea of a grassroots, mustard-seed covenant with the "outs" and the "outsiders" appears also in the parable of the leaven (yeast). But the depths of the parable lay in its use of mustard as a metaphor for "Emmanuel," the inauguration of the ongoing incarnational presence of God on earth.

The seed sown is the "seed" of the Word, the living Christ implanted within each disciple through the indwelling of the Spirit. You can trust the seed to reproduce at an astounding rate, taking over fields and propagating flowers.

> **MORE BAD HABITS**
>
> **Spent the first 30 years of his life doing nothing.**
> **JIM HENDERSON**

Jesus even mixes metaphors to have mustard seeds talking to mulberry trees: "If you had faith like a mustard seed, you would say to this mulberry tree, 'Be uprooted and be planted in the sea'; and it would obey you."[3] Life can be as diverse and extraordinary as the human imagination. The Jesus imagination enchants the world with a haunting presence—not that of leprechauns, gnomes, gremlins, and ghosts, but the haunting, gracing presence of the Holy Spirit, who can take the little and the taken-for-granted and make it large.

> With man this is impossible, but with God all things are possible.[4]

> This is what the LORD Almighty says: "It may seem marvelous [out of the ordinary] to the remnant of this people at that time, but will it seem marvelous [extraordinary] to me?[5]

We need this bad habit to kick in because the world's imagination authors a story line not formed by Kingdom virtues, values, and views. I grew up when the church was the scene of uncanny alchemy, the place where common things became uncommon, where grime turned to gold, where everyday events were infused with a sense of metaphysical moment. The atrophy of the church's imagination is one of the untold stories of the last few decades. But when the imagination soars, that's when the insults and assaults start in earnest.

It is not great numbers or great giftedness that "wins" for Jesus. In the strange, upside-down world of Jesus, the "win" is yielding into God's control the little, the ugly, and the unacceptable. In fact, giftedness, like riches, can be a hindrance when it leads to self-sufficiency rather than God-dependency.[6]

One of the strangest stories in the Gospels is known as "St. Peter's Fish" or "Peter's Penny." The fish in question is what we today know as tilapia, a fish common in the Sea of Galilee whose mouth was big enough to hold a coin.

The story goes like this: a Jewish law requires every Jew over nineteen years of age to pay each spring half a shekel, a double drachma (a Phoenician coin), to the Temple to maintain its upkeep. Collectors ask Peter if Jesus intends to pay the Temple tax. Peter impulsively says yes, but then spends some private time with Jesus explaining what he's done. Jesus claims tax-exempt status for his disciples. Priests and rabbis claimed to be free from the obligations of paying the Temple tax. Princes don't pay state taxes because of their relation to the king. Priests and rabbis don't pay Temple taxes because of their relation to God.

But Jesus says that even though his disciples have the right and freedom *not* to pay taxes to either church or state, they will not exercise their freedom so as not to cause offense. The liberty of community is limited for the sake of the outside community. So Peter pays the tax for Jesus and himself after he finds a "stater" (a one-shekel coin, or four drachmas) in a fish he has caught. This is enough to pay for both Peter and Jesus, implying that all Jesus' disciples will pay it generally, including Jewish Christians.

This is not a story about a strange fish. This is a story about Jesus' attitude toward political and social power. And this is a story about how God works through the natural to do the supernatural. When told to pay the tax, Peter does what he always does; he does what comes naturally; he does what he's trained to do: go fishing. God works through what comes naturally—catching fish—and God blesses those efforts. The natural isn't changed into the supernatural. The natural *is* the supernatural. Jesus was always infusing and suffusing the natural with a sense of holiness and infusing and suffusing the holy with a sense of the natural.

When Peter looked at life's waves and braced himself for the winds, taking his eyes off the Master of the winds and waves, he sank. So do we. If Jesus is not present, we will sink deeper and deeper into the morass into which humanity has fallen. If Jesus is present, the morass will still be there. The winds and the waves will still rage. But the sublime will be there alongside the slime; the silence will calm amid the storms and squalls.

There is no flawless masterpiece. Every life hits potholes. You can get down and dirty and tell a life story from the pits and potholes. Or you can keep your eyes on the main road and tell a life story from where it's headed. Jesus never leads us into dead ends. We find those on our own. Jesus leads us into the Way that is Life and Truth, which sometimes involves roundabouts and cul-de-sacs but not dead ends.

Jesus glowed, but not from a halo around his head, or some dressed-for-success attire. Jesus looked ordinary, but he glowed from the ordinary. Jesus showed his full solidarity with the common people even in how he looked and dressed and acted. Jesus did not exceed the forty days' fast of Moses or Elijah, lest we imagine him as some kind of superman or pretend human.[7]

> ## MORE BAD HABITS
>
> **We tend to admire people who get things done with no margin in their lives. Jesus had a bad habit of creating margin to have "margin"al encounters with marginalized people.**
>
> **ALLEN SOUTHERLAND**

Nobody celebrates the common man and woman more than Jesus. Wherever Jesus looked, he didn't see *massa damnata* (masses of the damned); he saw *massa dilectis Dei* (masses of God's beloved). And he called *massa dilectis Dei* to be the *plebs sancta Dei*—the holy common people of God. Jesus' love for the common people and the common life is evident everywhere in his stories that were themselves told in the colloquial and the vernacular. Jesus loved to tell stories that captured the ordinary moments of life in flagrante delicto, like those enduring images of Pompeii that are perfect monuments to the ordinary moments of everyday life. He tells of fishermen sorting fish, merchants searching for pearls, farmers plowing fields and harvesting crops, day laborers separating wheat from darnel, lepers begging food, shepherds minding flocks, women mending clothes, parents throwing parties, children playing games, kids fighting in village greens, women kneading dough, neighbors borrowing foodstuffs, burglars plundering homes, debtors struggling to pay loans, stewards managing households, young men leaving home for greener pastures, lovers getting married. In every Jesus story the numinous is in the normal, the holy haunts the mundane, the minuscule can be magisterial. In some ways Jesus the storyteller is postsemiotic in that his narratives escape all ulterior associations to set up residence only in the ordinary. A Jesus story is nothing but ordinary and about the sacredness of the ordinary.

The most common, obvious, plentiful things in life—water, earth, wind, light, trees, people—are the most valuable things, and the most scarce things in life—gems, gold, expensive garments—are the most worthless. Take away the most scarce, and how damaging is it? Take away the most common, and see where the value lies? We take off our shoes, not just to show respect for the sacredness of the moment but to show we're home where we belong and to celebrate our homecoming.

Jesus has the imagination of a gardener. Gardening is the ultimate collaboration between nature and nurture, between praise and prowess, between free and formal, between divine wild-work and human artwork. Jesus has the bad habit of celebrating the folk wisdom of the common people. He does not have the imagination of a craftsman or carpenter but an earthy imagination that works from below, builds from the bottom up, rather than deducing from the top down. Jesus has a tactile imagination that lets his hearers draw general conclusions from concrete cases—the small particulars of life. He does not tickle the fancy of his hearers so much as trigger their imaginations to take his stories to the next level in their own minds.

MORE BAD HABITS 💬

He believed ordinary people could do extraordinary things, and entrusted his ministry to people with issues and failings who wouldn't pass most HR screenings.

DAVID SWISHER

A Promethean imagination twists and turns the world into the shape of an "I." A Jesus imagination turns the world into the shape of a heart, where every common thing in every common day is related to all things extraordinary and glorious—like joy, beauty, goodness, truth, peace, and love.

Jesus' favorite time to pray was at dawn and dusk, the very

time God walked in the Garden of Eden with Adam and Eve. Why did Jesus love to walk the garden in the dew of the day? Because that's when animals and all creation come alive. Go to the zoo in the middle of the day, and all the animals are sleeping. The zenith of the day is "pit in the p.m.," when your body wants to siesta. But go on safari at dawn and dusk, and everything comes alive.

Jesus watches lilies, tracks ravens, climbs mountains, walks fields, lounges at seasides, escapes to deserts. He doesn't romanticize nature or sentimentalize its beauty. He just luxuriates in creation and relishes the food and fruit that come from it. Jesus loves the wisdom sayings of sailors (e.g., "Red sky in morning, sailors take warning; red sky at night, sailors delight").[8] Jesus knows the world of resource management and conservation, what we used to call "husbandry," backward and forward:

> He knew that sheep could easily stray into the wilderness, that farmers fatten calves for special feasts, and that donkeys and oxen should be taken every day to water. At times these animals would fall down wells and needed to be rescued at once, even on the Sabbath day. Jesus noted that cultivating the soil and adding fertiliser could revitalise barren fig trees. Farmers might buy up to five yoke of oxen. Gentile farmers kept pigs and fed them on pods. Jesus became familiar too with the market price of sparrows, the skins used for different brands of wine,

the safe places above the flood-line for constructing large buildings, and with weather forecasting. Winds from the West blow off the Mediterranean and bring rain; those from the South come off the desert and will be hot and dry.[9]

Frank Sinatra turned every drink he shared into what for him was a eucharistic moment. He would take the toothpick with two olives on it from his martini, offer one to the person who was eating or drinking with him, and invite the other person to throw the olive into his or her mouth with him. Bill Zehme in his book *The Way You Wear Your Hat: Frank Sinatra and the Lost Art of Livin'* (1999) calls this "something of a sacred act." What are you doing to turn your eating and drinking into sacred moments with others?

Stephen Hawking may be the smartest person alive today. He is a theoretical physicist, cosmologist, and the director of research at the Centre for Theoretical Cosmology at the University of Cambridge. When Hawking considers the vastness of the universe and how humans "are such insignificant creatures on a minor planet of a very average star in the outer suburbs of one of a hundred thousand million galaxies," he concludes, "It is difficult to believe in a God that would care about us."[10] The psalmist makes the same observation: "When I look at the night sky and see the work of your fingers—the moon and the stars you set in place—what are mere mortals that you should think about them, human beings that you should care for them?" But the psalmist's conclusion is the exact opposite of Hawking's: "Yet you made them only a little lower than God and crowned them with glory and honor."[11] How extraordinary, given our insignificance, that life should be so full of wonders and consolations.

JESUS THOUGHT HE
WAS GOD

CHAPTER FIFTEEN

JESUS' FAVORITE WAY of describing himself was as *Adam Kadmon*, most often translated "Son of Man" but best translated "the Human One." Jesus is not some ideal human being but the first true human being, the human being we were all created to be, whose resurrection makes the future our present. Baptism is not membership in the Christian church but membership in a whole new and pure line of being human and participation in the sacrament of humanity.

But Jesus also had this bad habit of describing himself as God and claiming a special relationship with God. For example:

- Jesus said he existed before Abraham.[1]
- Jesus said he was present at the beginning of Creation, and that "without Him was not anything made that was made."[2]
- Jesus said God was his Father, 120 times in John alone.
- Jesus said he had been sent "from above" into this world "below" by his Father.[3]
- Jesus said to see him was to see God.[4]
- Jesus said he could forgive sins.[5]
- Jesus said he could grant eternal life.[6]
- Jesus said he was the same as God: to know him was to know God, to hear him was to hear God, to see him was to see God, to experience him was to experience God, to hate him was to hate God, and to honor him was to honor God.[7]

The first time we meet Jesus after his birth, he is age twelve, camping out at Jerusalem, attending Passover with his family. For a couple of days, Jesus goes missing. Instead of going back home with the rest of the family, Jesus hangs back without telling anyone so he can hang out in the Temple. When Mary and Joseph notice his absence from the entourage after getting halfway home, they immediately return to Jerusalem, where they find him in the Temple with the rabbis and priests, asking scriptural questions and probing theological issues. When his parents rebuke him for staying behind without telling them what he was doing, he sasses back with a sequence of questions: "Why were you searching for me? . . . Didn't you know I had to be in my Father's house?"[8]

There it is. In question form, Jesus is asserting as a twelve-year-old that somehow his life is at the same time caught up in the very life of God. Jesus' Abba experiences were ones of immediacy and intimacy: immediate access to God and intimate awareness of God.

Even as a twelve-year-old, Jesus showed how he didn't just give question answers; he gave answer questions. One time Jesus asked this question: "Whose son is Jesus Christ?" When he responded to the Pharisees' answer with another question, "no one dared ask him any more questions."[9] No one knew exactly how to answer someone who thought he was God.

From the very beginning Jesus had this bad habit of claiming a special Father-Son relationship with God. No

MORE BAD HABITS

Jesus broke up every funeral he attended, including his own.

DAVID DELOZIER

doubt this grew in acuteness and astuteness throughout his life, but throughout the Gospel narratives, Jesus annoyed the religious authorities with his pretentious assertions of a special relationship with God that took the form of forgiving sins, healing the sick, exorcising demons, touching the unclean, and raising the dead. But this special relationship with God that Jesus claimed for himself was special in that it renounced specialness. You see this in the two angelic announcements of his special birth: one to a priest in the Temple, the other to a young virgin from a nowhere place known for not-nice people. The way of the Messiah is the way of the cross. And the way of the cross leads home, but the way of the cross passes through the valleys of humility and ambiguity and obscurity and hostility. That's some specialness!

James Joyce only half-jokingly declared that "the demand I make of my reader is that he should devote his whole life to reading my works." Jesus had the bad habit of making a similar demand of his disciples: that they devote their whole lives to following him. In story and sign and speech, Jesus said in a variety of ways, "You aren't complete—the person God created you to be—until you find yourself in me."

Imagine someone today saying, "When you know me, in all my fullness and glory, you will know all you need to know."

Imagine someone today saying, "Life is not an individual project. Life is an intervidual pilgrimage where we all share my mission together."

Today Jesus would be diagnosed as suffering not just from delusions of grandeur, but from the worst mental condition you can have: a God complex.

The two temptations of Jesus, the temptations of the wilderness and the garden,[10] are where Jesus' divine consciousness is most apparent. In the wilderness, Jesus knows he is the Messiah. The only question is what kind of Messiah he will be. Will he be the world's kind of Messiah or the Kingdom's kind of Messiah? Will he be a Messiah who uses power—economic power, military and political power, religious power—or a Messiah who uses beauty and truth and goodness? Will the peak of his ministry be a political, economic, or social crusade? Or will the apex and climax of Jesus' ministry be a Golgotha cross, garden tomb, and gathering cloud: the Tree, the Tomb, the Throne?

It was as hard for Jesus' contemporaries to receive this truth as it is for us today. The eternal gospel is not some pure precipitate of the core of all religions. The eternal gospel is not some rarified teaching of the highest moral precepts like you find in the Sermon on the Mount. The eternal gospel is . . . Jesus.

Everyone knows John 3:16. But there is another verse like it. It's found in the other John, 1 John 4:10: "This is love: not that we loved God, but that he loved us and sent his Son as an atoning sacrifice for our sins." In other words, the greatest love story ever told, the love story that stops clocks and starts hearts, is a love story that began in heaven and brought heaven's best to us, to begin heaven in us, to spread heaven among us, to prepare us for heaven as heaven prepares for us. Heaven has a name: Jesus Christ.

That's why preachers of the gospel preach so that you carry not the preachers' words in your head, but Jesus' stories and metaphors in your mind and heart. The church is off course and missing her course because she has not stayed the course with Jesus but strayed into courses on a hundred other subjects.

Isaac, the son of the promise, has the wood laid on his shoulder and climbs the mount at the will of his father. Jesus, the Son of God, has the olive-wood cross laid on his shoulder and climbs the mount at the will of his Father. Isaac said to his father Abraham, "The fire and wood are here, but where is the lamb for the burnt offering?" Abraham said, "God himself will provide the lamb for the burnt offering, my son."[11]

The real glory of Jesus is up on the mountain, his passion and death on Golgotha, where God provided the Lamb for the salvation of the world. There is only one answer to the problem of suffering and pain in life. The answer is not a theodicy or a philosophy. The answer is not some comforting words or proverbs or platitudes. The answer is the story of Jesus, the Son of God, who suffered and died on the cross.

> **MORE BAD HABITS**
>
> **The only person to be devoid of a messiah complex was the Messiah.**
>
> **VERN HYNDMAN**

If all we had was Paul's writings, we would know almost nothing of the words or teachings of Jesus.[12] Paul is not at all interested in red-lettering the earthly Jesus. What does interest Paul—in fact, totally consumes Paul's mind, body, and spirit—is what Jesus *did*. Jesus was born. Jesus was crucified. Jesus was raised from the dead. Jesus will come again. In contrast to the Gnostic Gospels, where all that matters is the teachings of Jesus, all that really matters for Paul is Jesus the dying, rising, and returning Savior. This is equally true for any of the other New Testament writings—James, Jude, Peter, and even the non-epistolary, narrative text of Revelation. The focus is more on what Jesus did, less on what Jesus said.

Jill Briscoe tells of a visit to a funeral home with a grieving widow, standing by the open casket. Out of the corner of her eye, Jill sees a member of her church coming toward them and thinks, *Here comes trouble*. The woman approaching the casket believes Christians should never be sad or weep; they should always be upbeat and happy. Predictably, the dear lady comes up and starts to comfort the grieving widow with words about thinking positively and lifting the chin. The widow looks at her and says, "Well, if we are not supposed to cry, how come Jesus wept?" Whereupon Jill, with her wonderful British wit, says, "Well obviously, honey, Jesus wasn't a very good Christian."

Wait a minute! Jesus, not a very good Christian? Come to think of it, he would not be, based on some of our definitions.

Jesus was not a very good Christian if by "good Christian" we mean someone who is respectable, presentable, well mannered, well meaning, and well wishing.

Jesus was not a very good Christian if by "good Christian" we mean someone who moves in gospel goose step at authority's command.

Jesus was not a very good Christian if by "good Christian" we mean the business of getting more things, if the gospel is "good news" about increasing our living standards more than our loving standards.

Jesus was not a very good Christian if by "good Christian" we mean the sort of person who is always snooping around to see if people are enjoying themselves and then trying to stop it.

Jesus was not a very good Christian if by "good Christian" we mean disciples of the doctrines of Jesus, not disciples of Jesus.

Jesus was not a very good Christian if by "good Christian" we mean someone who tries to save the standing order rather than creating an alternative order of reality within every standing order.

Jesus was not a very good Christian if by "good Christian" we mean always being a "winner." For Jesus, you can be a "winner" without someone else losing or without having all your demands met.

Jesus was not a very good Christian if by "good Christian" we mean a gravy train for the professionals.

Jesus was not a very good Christian if by "good Christian" we mean someone who has the right friends and keeps the right kind of company. Jesus hung not with the "in" crowd but with the sinners, while the pious and the hypocrites watched from the wings and criticized. Are we commingling or criticizing? And at Calvary, he literally hung with the sinners in dying as he hung with them in living.

Jesus was not a very good Christian if by "good Christian" we mean someone who has a problem with sin. Sin is not a problem for Jesus. The problem is getting sinners to see they are sinners, confess their separation from God, and accept God's invitation.

Jesus was not a very good Christian if by "good Christian"

we mean someone who hears the voice of Jesus as but an echo of the culture's voices and not a voice from beyond. Zeitgeist is not *Heilige Geist*.

Jesus was not a very good Christian if by "good Christian" we mean an algorithmic, step-by-step, predictable approach to church, life, and mission. Jesus said his disciples would be born of water and of wind, and "you cannot tell where [the wind] comes from or where it is going. So it is with everyone born of the Spirit."[13]

MORE BAD HABITS

He obeyed his Father.

DAVID ARNOLD

Jesus was not a very good Christian if by "good Christian" we mean someone who never got angry or upset. Jesus was the enfant terrible of the Temple.

Jesus was not a very good Christian if by "good Christian" we mean someone who constantly shares everything God is doing in her or his life. In fact, Jesus did some miracles and wanted everyone to keep quiet about it.

Jesus was not a very good Christian if by "good Christian" we mean someone who would like to be labeled "Christian" or "good." "Why do you call me good?" Jesus answered the rich man. "Only God is truly good."[14]

Jesus wants to be the most rewritten character in history. He wants his story to be rewritten in your life. The story of Christianity is the story of how people are rewriting the Jesus story in their own lives. Look around you, and see how people are finding Jesus in their own lives and writing his story in new script. Aquinas said that wherever there is beauty and truth and goodness, there is Jesus.

When Jesus becomes the plot that pilots the story, when Jesus becomes the thread that seams together the nature and nurture of life, your life story becomes a masterpiece. Philosophy may be "a series of footnotes to Plato," in the opinion of Alfred North Whitehead, but to live an abundant life means each one of our lives is a series of footnotes to Jesus. The church is the people who live Jesus. All of Jesus, even the bad-habits Jesus. Not the people who remember Jesus, but the people who experience, embody, and evidence Jesus' resurrection life. When you know Jesus, in all his fullness and glory, you will know all you need to know. *Yada*, *Yada*, *Yada*: The Unknown (God) made Known (Jesus) for us to Know (Holy Spirit). When you live Jesus, in all his abundance and brilliance, you will do more than mimic Jesus; you will manifest Jesus. And when you manifest Jesus, there will be a tangible, palpable presencing of Jesus in the world.[15]

BREAKING BAD

CONCLUSION

THIS IS FUNDAMENTALLY A BOOK about the Incarnation.
Where does the Incarnation fit in terms of theology? Most
see it in terms of soteriology (salvation) or eschatology (end
times). But I think it properly belongs within the frame-
work of Creation. The consummation of the original act of
Creation was the once-for-all-time incarnation in Jesus and
the ongoing incarnation of that once-for-all-time incarnation
in each and every one of us. If Jesus had not left but stayed,
he would have kept inside him what was in him. That Jesus
left us and sent us the Holy Spirit meant that what was inside
him was let out and now is inside us.[1]

That means Jesus left us both his good and his bad habits. And in Jesus' day he was most known for being bad, not good. The religious establishment of Jesus' day were good—no, they were great. In fact, there was nobody better at keeping a list than the Pharisees were. The problem was they were so good, they thought they had it all wrapped up. Today, too, far too many churches are filled with people who are unrecognizable as Jesus' followers due to their lack of Jesus' bad habits!

Jesus was a master at challenging convention and the status quo. But he was also a master at healing brokenness. If you want to incarnate Jesus in your life and in your church, you need to quit tallying up your "good" behavior and try a few of Jesus' bad habits!

One of Jesus' worst habits was to be everything to everybody. A Kentucky holiness evangelist and educator named W. B. Dunkum wrote a little book about this called *The Man of Galilee* that became a holiness classic and went through multiple editions. He litanized this bad habit based on Jesus' names in the Bible. It was picked up and popularized in various sources.

Based on Jesus' question to Peter, "Who do you say that I am?" Dunkum provided answers:

To the artist . . . Jesus is the One altogether lovely.
To the architect . . . Jesus is the Chief Cornerstone.
To the astronomer . . . Jesus is the Sun of Righteousness.
To the baker . . . Jesus is the Living Bread.

To the banker . . . Jesus is the Hidden Treasure.

To the biologist . . . Jesus is the Life.

To the builder . . . Jesus is the Strong and Sure Foundation.

To the carpenter . . . Jesus is the Door.

To the doctor . . . Jesus is the Great Physician.

To the educator . . . Jesus is the Great Teacher.

To the engineer . . . Jesus is the New and Living Way.

To the farmer . . . Jesus is the Sower and Lord of the Harvest.

To the florist . . . Jesus is the Rose of Sharon, Lily of the Valley.

To the geologist . . . Jesus is the Rock of Ages.

To the horticulturist . . . Jesus is the True Vine.

To the judge . . . Jesus is the Righteous Judge, Judge of All.

To the juror . . . Jesus is the Faithful and True Witness.

To the jeweler . . . Jesus is the Pearl of Great Price.

To the lawyer . . . Jesus is the Counselor, Lawgiver, Advocate.

To the journalist . . . Jesus is the Good Tidings of Great Joy.

To the optometrist . . . Jesus is the Light of the Eyes.

To the philanthropist . . . Jesus is the Unspeakable Gift.

To the philosopher . . . Jesus is the Wisdom of God.

To the preacher . . . Jesus is the Word of God.

To the sculptor . . . Jesus is the Living Stone.

To the servant . . . Jesus is the Good Master.

To the statesman . . . Jesus is the Desire of All Nations.

To the student . . . Jesus is the Incarnate Truth.

To the theologian . . . Jesus is the Author and Finisher of Faith.

To the toiler . . . Jesus is the Giver of Rest.

To the sinner . . . Jesus is the Lamb of God that takes away the sins of the world.

To the Christian . . . Jesus is the Son of the Living God, the Savior, the Redeemer, and Lord.[2]

To you and me, Jesus is the Human One as well as the Son of God, the same as you and me but with the kinds of outstanding bad habits that made his heavenly Father proud—bad habits that we would do well to learn. It is not good habits that recharge the church. It is bad habits and unconventional approaches that recharge tradition.

May we make all his habits our own.

ABOUT THE AUTHOR

LEONARD SWEET has authored more than 1,500 published sermons, 200 articles, and 60 books, including most recently *The Well-Played Life*, *From Tablet to Table*, and the groundbreaking preaching text *Giving Blood: A Fresh Paradigm for Preaching*. Leonard has been named one of the 50 Most Influential Christians in America by the *Church Report* magazine, and his microblogs on Twitter and Facebook are rated as two of the most influential social media accounts in the world. Dr. Sweet is the E. Stanley Jones Professor of Evangelism at Drew Theological School at Drew University and Visiting Distinguished Professor at George Fox Evangelical Seminary and at Tabor College. Leonard is the premier writer and owner of the fast-growing, innovative preaching resource www.preachthestory.com.

DISCUSSION GUIDE

CHAPTER 1: JESUS SPIT

1. This chapter references John 9, where Jesus heals a man who was born blind. The author writes, "Imagine the shock—or perhaps not—when Jesus faced the man and spat upon the ground. Perhaps everyone around him was nodding in approval, thinking that Jesus was obviously showing his contempt for the outcast Jew" (page 4). Picture yourself in this scene. What do you think you would be doing? What do you think you might say to the person standing next to you?

2. The author writes, "You can't up-up-and-away in creativity and innovation without spending down-on-the-ground time in the muck and mire" (page 6). What would you identify as "muck and mire" in your own culture? Have there been times when God has asked you to spend time in the "muck and mire"? Can you identify creativity or growth or relationships cultivated or change stimulated that has emerged from that time spent "down on the ground"? What kind of creative

changes have you observed emerging from others who
have spent time with unexpected people or in expected
places?

3. After reading the story of Jesus healing a man born
   blind (John 9), compare the healed man's response
   to Jesus' and the Pharisees' responses. What are the
   differences? Which response do you relate to more?
   Why? How does this story point to Jesus as Son
   of God?

CHAPTER 2: JESUS PROCRASTINATED

1. Procrastination could be considered a bad habit, but
   Christians are "sent to do things we had no intention
   of doing or to go places we had no intention of going
   or to meet people we had no intention of meeting"
   (page 18). Can you describe any such times in your life,
   when you stepped into God's time zone and stepped
   out of your own? What was the result? What can we
   learn from Jesus' procrastination in reaching those
   in a panic about their loved ones? What does Jesus'
   procrastination tell us about the nature of prayer?

2. The author writes, "Jesus is the most creative person
   who ever lived. His life, death, and resurrection are the
   very definitions of creativity. The most creative acts in
   history are God-generated acts. It shouldn't surprise us
   that creative people are often chronic procrastinators"
   (page 18). What is your reaction to this? Does it change
   the way you think of Jesus' life, death, and resurrection?

How might it change the way you share the gospel message?

3. The author writes, "The church is so busy about so many things. We would be well advised to learn Jesus' bad habit of procrastination. We especially need to learn to wait on Jesus, which has both a Martha and a Mary meaning" (page 22). Who are the Marthas and Marys in your church? In what ways are they waiting on Jesus? How does the Mary and Martha story describe faith and fellowship in both of these women?

CHAPTER 3: JESUS APPEARED WASTEFUL

1. Jesus was accused of being a drunkard and a glutton (which might seem preposterous, or at least not fitting, to contemporary readers of the Bible). He was accused of wasting his time and his reputation on "sinners" (see page 26). Have you experienced times when "wastefulness" has contributed to ministry? Explain.

2. The author writes, "God has created life and all creation with plenitude, not scarcity. A scarcity mind-set is either-or thinking; a plenitude mind-set is both-and, and-also thinking" (page 29). In considering the story of Mary pouring expensive perfume over Jesus' feet in John 12:1-8, why does Jesus commend her wastefulness? In what ways can we "pour out" our praise to Jesus in our worship communities?

3. The author writes, "Jesus is a bad planner. He makes too much wine. He makes too much food. . . .

Jesus does not have an economics of scarcity, but an economics of abundance" (page 30). Consider the needs you have encountered recently in your world (in your city, your church, your neighborhood). Name one or two ways you could be a "bad planner" in meeting the needs of those in your community and operating from the economics of abundance.

CHAPTER 4: JESUS WAS CONSTANTLY DISAPPEARING

1. The author writes, "The more plugged in and connected we are, the more we need to unplug and disconnect. . . . Perhaps this is also the best definition of prayer: the times when we disappear from our busyness and our pressing chores and spend time in God's presence, just as Jesus did" (pages 48, 50). Do you have a set time every day that you spend in solitude and prayer with God? Can you describe times in life when you've been able to do that consistently? If you have gotten out of the "bad habit" of disappearing, can you make a plan to schedule disappearances at some point in your day, every day, for the next seven days? And then the seven days after that? "The more you do it, the more . . . your life will look . . . like a beautiful manifestation of Jesus" (page 52).

2. In this chapter, the author mentions another of Jesus' bad habits: "his imposing on others and inviting himself in" (page 50). Have there been occasions, situations, or conversations that you perhaps avoided talking about

Jesus because you didn't want to "impose"? How did you feel about your decision to not impose? Conversely, can you describe a time when you did impose? What was the outcome?

3. Describe a time when someone may have "imposed" on you in a way that allowed you to see Jesus in a new way. The author says, "Jesus wants his followers to turn imposition into opportunity by seizing it" (page 51). Seizing opportunities may mean talking about Jesus at times and places other than in the church on Sundays. How can you or your church create new opportunities to "get out of doors" in order to point to Jesus in the world and in other people's lives in ways they may not expect?

CHAPTER 5: JESUS OFFENDED PEOPLE, ESPECIALLY IN HIGH PLACES

1. Have you offended anyone lately by living out your faith in public? What was your experience? Are you ashamed to speak of Jesus in a non-Jesus culture? How can you love someone who thinks differently than you do while still allowing Jesus to live his life in yours?

2. What are some ways we can practice and communicate in our daily lives "critical discernment, moral judgment, and compassionate evaluation of what brings life and what brings death . . . in a world in which everyone is easily offended or playing defense" (page 58, 60–61)?

3. The author ends this chapter with "The very meaning of love [is] to be provoked by suffering and injustice

and inhumanity. To follow Jesus is to be provoked
. . . and provocative. If we are to live out Christ in
the world, we need to get rid of our fear of offending
people and get on with Christ's mission in the
world" (page 66). What kind of suffering, injustice,
or inhumanity provokes you the most? What kinds
of ministry would address this kind of pain in your
community? How can your church offer provocative
ministry that initiates change?

CHAPTER 6: JESUS TOLD STORIES THAT DIDN'T MAKE SENSE

1. Try this exercise. Imagine yourself in a crowd of people
   as Jesus is telling a parable. Pick a parable each day
   to read from the Gospels, picturing yourself listening
   as you are standing next to Muslims, to agnostics, to
   immigrants, to politicians, and to your family members
   and friends. What do you think each of their reactions
   would be to Jesus? What is your reaction? Which
   parables of Jesus resonate most with you? Why?

2. The author asserts that Jesus told stories that didn't
   make sense. They always had an unusual twist.
   Discuss the parable of the prodigal son (see Luke
   15:11-32). What are the unusual twists in the story
   that people would not be expecting? How has Jesus
   shocked his listeners in this story? Do the same with
   the parable of Lazarus and the rich man (see Luke
   16:19-31).

3. The author says, "You can't escape living in and

through a story. All of us are living a story. The question is what story and whose story are you living? Madison Avenue? Wall Street? Hollywood? Or Bethlehem?" (page 77). What does it look like to be living in each story? What does it look like to live Jesus' story?

CHAPTER 7: JESUS LOVED TO PARTY

1. The author asks, "Are we missing golden opportunities to influence popular culture because we are afraid to be seen having fun?" (page 81). Have you ever been afraid of being seen having too much fun? Have there been times when you have felt guilty for having fun? Why do you think you had those feelings? Where might they have come from?

2. The author says, "Jesus teaches us that the party habit could be the best way to break the ice and influence even the seediest of characters" (pages 81–82). Can you describe any instances of this in your life, as the one who either has influenced others through fun or has been influenced by others' "party habits"?

3. The author writes, "The church above all should be a place of festivities and joy. People should look at the church and think, *What joyful people!* If more of the church shared Jesus' bad habit of loving to party, it would be the place everyone would want to be" (page 87). What are some ideas to make your church "a place of festivities and joy"? How about your home?

CHAPTER 8: JESUS COULD BE DANGEROUS

1. "Wrong interpretations [of Scripture] can yield pharisaical commitment to practices and rituals rather than to the person of Jesus. But true faith that walks the talk and toes the line of true discipleship can be downright dangerous," the author writes (page 92). What "pharisaical practices" have you or your church found yourself participating in rather than walking with Jesus in true discipleship? What happens when rituals and habits become more important than a relationship with Jesus?

2. On page 97, the author writes, "Can we ditch old dreams and hitch new hopes to imaginative horizons that find their home in the dangerous habits of Christ? It's the only way for us to be dangerous and contagious again." What old dreams or stale habits do you or your church need to ditch in order to live dangerously and contagiously? What do you need to *let* go of (see page 99) and *let* God do? What would a contagious church look like in your community and in your world?

CHAPTER 9: JESUS HUNG OUT WITH BAD PEOPLE

1. The author says, "The more our relationships are linked socially and emotionally with diverse others, the richer and fuller life will be" (page 104). What does this statement mean to you? Many churches spend most of their time in relationship with each other, and those coming into the church are expected to become like

those within it. How can you encourage your church to be more open to differences in preference, in people, in style, and in worship? How can you encourage your church to spend more time with people in your community whom they have never met? How can you create opportunities in which to build relationships with people who have not yet met Jesus?

2. What experiences in ministry outside of the church have made you flinch? Why? How can you begin to feel comfortable with others who are unlike you?

3. The author says, "We are also called to follow some we don't think are worthy of God's anointing" (page 107). Have you been called to serve, or to work with, people who may seem to you unworthy of God's anointing? How did or how do you respond?

CHAPTER 10: JESUS SPENT TOO MUCH TIME WITH CHILDREN

1. "Jesus made faith child friendly and adult averse, meaning Jesus did everything he could to protect children's faith from adults and to help even the most adultish among us become more childlike" (pages 114–115). Think about some children you know. What is it about them that Jesus so admired? What can you learn from the children in your church?

2. The author says, "Many of our churches today banish children to distant parts of the building during worship, then bemoan their absence from church when these same kids reach adulthood. Instead of Jesus'

'Let the children come unto me,' the church says, 'Let us babysit your kids while we dazzle you adults in worship'" (page 114). What are your thoughts about this? Do you think there are more ways your church could or should involve children in worship services? Is there something you can do to help with that?

3. The author says in this chapter that stories build identity. How can you practice telling the stories of Jesus not just in your church but in your home, in your parenting, in your actions, in your everyday life?

CHAPTER 11: JESUS EITHER TALKED TOO MUCH OR WAS SILENT WHEN HE SHOULD HAVE TALKED

1. "Jesus seemed either to be talking when he should have been silent or silent when he should have been talking. When his life depended on him saying nothing, he said something. When his life depended on him saying something, he said nothing," writes the author (page 129). Describe a time in your own life when silence was the best thing to say.

2. On page 132, the author talks about living the life of faith, "living the mystery." He writes about Jesus talking in gestures and the fact that "Jesus refused to get entangled in words." How do we incorporate "living the mystery" in our world today? In what ways does your worship service create an atmosphere in which you can revel or marinate in the mysteriousness of God? Describe a time when you had no answer for

something but had to simply trust in the providence and grace of God.

CHAPTER 12: JESUS BROKE THE RULES

1. The author writes, "Jesus would break the rules to bless you" (page 139). Ponder that for a moment. How do you feel when you read that? The author also writes on page 139, "A Jesus world was a world turned upside down." Can you remember a time in your church or in your parenting when you broke the rules in order to bless or forgive or comfort someone? In our society and in our churches, some rules are God's rules and must be respected (such as "do not kill"). Other rules are of lesser importance, such as where to place the candles or what music is allowed to be played in church. What rules are you willing to break in order to foster new relationships and create innovative ministry in your church?

2. "Jesus' bad habit of rule breaking is a lesson for our own relationships. To reject someone's idea gets often conveyed as a rejection or condemnation of that person. Can we think someone wrong and still be in right relationship with them?" writes the author on pages 142–143. What is your answer to that question? Describe a time when you experienced this dilemma.

3. "Today's churches need to cultivate Jesus' bad habit of breaking some traditions and rules and living in such a way that makes the heart sing and the mind dance"

(page 144). Name one tradition or rule in your church that you think could or should be broken in order to "make the heart sing and the mind dance." What would it look like for your church to abolish this rule?

CHAPTER 13: JESUS ENJOYED THE COMPANY OF WOMEN (NOT JUST MEN)

1. The author writes, "Imagine the pious outrage when Jesus touched an adolescent girl, a hemorrhaging woman, a Gentile female, and a woman he healed of demons" (page 152). In Jesus' day, women were not to be touched by a man in public. It was taboo. Now imagine Jesus today, visiting churches and gatherings and spending time with those considered to be taboo in contemporary society. Who are those people in your culture? What would you say to your friends and family about this person who claims to be Messiah and yet breaks so many traditions and rules?

2. On page 156, the author notes that after Jesus' resurrection, he appears to Mary Magdalene and tells her to report this to the disciples. Why do you think Jesus did this, "when a woman's testimony would have been worthless"?

CHAPTER 14: JESUS FOCUSED ON THE LITTLE THINGS IN LIFE

1. On page 165, the author writes, "Jesus did not mount campaigns against the social structures of his day but focused on the needs of neighbors and individuals." What are three ways that your church can begin to

build relationships and ministries that address the
needs of neighbors and individuals in your community?

2. "You find God in the midst: the midst of the everyday,
the midst of the mundane, the midst of the obvious"
(page 166). What "little" could you put "into the hands
of the one who holds the world in hand and see little
become large"? (Or, put another way, the author asks,
"What's your 0.2 percent?") Name at least one small
thing you can do or have done—something everyday,
mundane, or obvious—in the name of Jesus to bless
someone in your life. Do you have a story of something
someone did in your life that impacted who you have
become?

3. The author asks, "What are you doing to turn your
eating and drinking into sacred moments with others?"
(page 174). What are you doing, or what could you
do? Use your imagination, remembering that "the
world's imagination authors a story line not formed
by Kingdom virtues, values, and views" and "when the
imagination soars, that's when the insults and assaults
start in earnest" (page 168). How often do you spend
time with others at the "table"? How can you make
your table time a sacred space for sharing, loving, and
imagining?

CHAPTER 15: JESUS THOUGHT HE WAS GOD

1. "Jesus is not some ideal human being but the first true
human being, the human being we were all created

to be," writes the author on page 179. Think about that description of Jesus for a moment. How does this description change the way you look at Jesus? How does this change the way you look at yourself?

2. Read page 185–187—"Jesus was not a very good Christian if by 'good Christian' we mean . . ." Does this description of Jesus differ from the way you have viewed what it means to be a Christian? In what ways?

3. The author ends this chapter with, "Jesus wants to be the most rewritten character in history. He wants his story to be rewritten in your life. The story of Christianity is the story of how people are rewriting the Jesus story in their own lives. Look around you, and see how people are finding Jesus in their own lives and writing his story in new script" (page 187–188). How are you seeing Jesus' story being written in new script in your life? In the lives of others around you? In your church?

CONCLUSION: BREAKING BAD

1. The author writes on page 192, "If you want to incarnate Jesus in your life and in your church, you need to quit tallying up your 'good' behavior and try a few of Jesus' bad habits!" Since starting this study, have you tried any of Jesus' bad habits? How did it go? If you haven't, which one would you like to try today?

NOTES

CHAPTER 1: JESUS SPIT

1. See Matthew 26:67.
2. See Leviticus 15:8; Numbers 12:14; Deuteronomy 25:9; Job 17:6; 30:10; Isaiah 50:6.
3. See John 9.
4. Genesis 2:5-7.
5. 1 John 3:2, RSV.
6. See Genesis 2:7; John 1:14. The word *adam* or *adama* means "dirt." The creation story is the ultimate incarnation. God speaks everything into existence, even Adam (made from the dirt of the earth and the waters of the deep).
7. Eric Velu, *Mama Heidi*, directed by Eric Velu (Eric Velu Productions, 2004).
8. See 1 Corinthians 15:45.
9. For example, "that saved a wretch like me" (John Newton's "Amazing Grace"); or "for such a worm as I" (Isaac Watts's "Alas! and Did My Savior Bleed").
10. See Isaiah 64:6.
11. See Philippians 4:13.
12. See Psalm 19:1.
13. Genesis 28:16.
14. Marvin R. Wilson, *Exploring our Hebraic Heritage: A Christian Theology of Roots and Renewal* (Grand Rapids, MI: Eerdmans, 2014), 194.
15. Matthew 18:20.
16. See Mark 10:46-52.

CHAPTER 2: JESUS PROCRASTINATED

1. See Revelation 4:8-10.
2. See Ephesians 5:16-17.
3. Ecclesiastes 8:6.
4. See Matthew 5:23-24.
5. See Ephesians 4:26.
6. See Luke 14:21.
7. Alfred Brendel, *Music, Sense and Nonsense: Collected Essays and Lectures* (London: Biteback Publishing, 2015).
8. Luke 14:28.
9. See Luke 12:50.
10. Luke 23:28-29, paraphrase.
11. See 1 Peter 5:7.

CHAPTER 3: JESUS APPEARED WASTEFUL

1. John 6:12, rsv.
2. Matthew 11:19; compare Luke 7:34.
3. See Matthew 14:15-20.
4. See Matthew 15:32-39.
5. See my book *From Tablet to Table* (Colorado Springs: NavPress, 2014).
6. Eusebius, *Church History*, bk. 7, chap. 22.
7. Howard V. Harper, "Stewardship—Accounting to God," *Beaver County Times*, November 11, 1961, https://news.google.com/newspapers?nid =2002&dat=19611111&id=W-0uAAAAIBAJ&sjid=dNsFAAAAIBAJ&pg =880,1801269&hl=en.
8. See Albion Barrera, *Economic Compulsion and Christian Ethics* (New York: Cambridge University Press, 2005).
9. As a bonus, scientific studies reveal that doing good could actually be good for you. For example, kidney donors live longer than average.
10. See Luke 16:1-13.
11. John 2:2.

CHAPTER 4: JESUS WAS CONSTANTLY DISAPPEARING

1. Matthew 28:19-20.
2. John 14:26.
3. John 5:19, 30.
4. See Genesis 2:18; Matthew 26:36-46.
5. "So I plan to stop off on my way to Spain. Then after a short, but refreshing, visit with you, I hope you will quickly send me on" (Romans 15:24, cev).

6. John 16:7.
7. See Luke 5:2; 19:29-35; 22:7-13; 23:50-53.

CHAPTER 5: JESUS OFFENDED PEOPLE, ESPECIALLY IN HIGH PLACES

1. Matthew 19:24; see Matthew 25:30.
2. John 8:55; Matthew 12:33-36; Matthew 23.
3. See Luke 13:32-33.
4. Matthew 16:22-24.
5. Jesus chose to put on his team Simon, a Zealot.
6. John 14:6.
7. Isaiah 53:5.
8. Edward Docx, *Self Help* (London: Pan Macmillan, 2007), 142.
9. For more on this, see Lynne Truss in *Talk to the Hand* (New York: Penguin, 2005), where she argues that "perceived rudeness probably irritates rough, insolent people even more than it peeves polite, deferential ones."
10. Søren Kierkegaard, *Works of Love* (New York: Harper & Row, 1962), 19.
11. Thomas Aquinas, *Summa Theologica*, Question 158, Article 1.
12. Julian of Norwich, quoted by Timothy Radcliffe, *Why Go to Church?: The Drama of the Eucharist* (London: Continuum, 2008), 18.
13. See Mark 3:2-6.
14. 1 Corinthians 13:5, KJV.

CHAPTER 6: JESUS TOLD STORIES THAT DIDN'T MAKE SENSE

1. See Luke 16:19-31.
2. See Luke 22:35-38.
3. Matthew 2:2.
4. Quoted in Colin Morris, *Things Shaken—Things Unshaken* (London: Epworth, 2006), 86.
5. See John 1:35-42.

CHAPTER 7: JESUS LOVED TO PARTY

1. Matthew 11:19.
2. Isaiah 53:3, RSV.
3. Rainer Maria Rilke, *Duino Elegies*, trans. J. B. Leishman and Stephen Spender (New York: Norton, 1963), 79.
4. Psalm 92:2, NASB.
5. Lamentations 3:21-23, NRSV.
6. Augustine, *Augustine's Commentary on Galatians*, trans. Eric Plumer (New York: Oxford University Press, 2003), 215.

CHAPTER 8: JESUS COULD BE DANGEROUS

1. Matthew 10:14.
2. For more, see 1 Peter 1:1-8.
3. Luke 1:44.
4. Colossians 3:16, RSV.
5. Philippians 2:5, KJV.
6. Luke 1:38, RSV.

CHAPTER 9: JESUS HUNG OUT WITH BAD PEOPLE

1. See Luke 8:27-39.
2. John Edward Terrell, Termeh Shafie, and Mark Golitko, "How Networks Are Revolutionizing Scientific (and Maybe Human) Thought," *Scientific American*, Guest Blog on December 12, 2014, http://blogs .scientificamerican.com/guest-blog/how-networks-are-revolutionizing -scientific-and-maybe-human-thought/.
3. John 4:18, CEV.
4. John 4:29.
5. Roman Catholicism is the ultimate oxymoron.
6. See Numbers 11:16-17, 24-30.
7. See Hosea 14:4-7.
8. See Jeremiah 3:14, KJV.

CHAPTER 10: JESUS SPENT TOO MUCH TIME WITH CHILDREN

1. See Mark 7:27; Matthew 19:14.
2. For more on the relationship between children and creativity, see my book *The Well-Played Life* (Carol Stream, IL: Tyndale Momentum, 2014).
3. See Lauren Caldwell, *There's No Junior Holy Spirit: A Supernatural Training Manual for Youth* (Sterling City, TX: Garden, 2011).
4. See Janetta Goldstein, "The Invisible Robe: An Alternative Ending to a Famous Tale," *Times Literary Supplement*, February 21, 2014, 15.
5. Carolyn Osiek and Margaret Y. MacDonald, "Giving Birth: Labor, Nursing, and the Care of Infants in House-Church Communities," *A Woman's Place: House Churches in Earliest Christianity* (Minneapolis: Fortress Press, 2006), 55–56. The succeeding centuries didn't improve much until the last fifty years. As recently as a hundred years ago, a woman going into labor had the same survival rate as a soldier going into a foxhole. Queen Anne of England (1665–1714) had seventeen pregnancies with only one child surviving past infancy and that one died at age eleven. My Appalachian grandmother (West Virginia) birthed fourteen children, only seven of which survived to adulthood. Life expectancy has remained relatively stable over the past

two thousand years. It's the infant mortality rates that have dramatically changed, improving the "average" life expectancy for both males and females.

6. Thanks to David Brown for this insight.

7. Children of college-educated parents receive 50 percent more "Goodnight Moon" time (as Robert Putnam calls it) than those without.

8. C. E. M. Joad, *God and Evil* (New York: Harper and Brothers,1943), 307.

9. See Mark 9:33-37; 10:35-45.

10. Luke 1:46, 52, esv. The New English Bible translates verse 52: "He has torn imperial powers from their thrones, but the humble have been lifted high."

11. David Bodanis, "A Core Decency Even the Worst Government Machinations Can't Hold Down," in *What Are You Optimistic About?*, ed. John Brockman (New York: Harper Perennial, 2007), 353.

12. Ephesians 4:14-15.

13. In this two-part interview titled "Grim Colberty Tales" with Maurice Sendak, recorded in January 2012, Sendak makes his last known video appearance.

14. C. S. Lewis, *On Stories: And Other Essays on Literature* (Orlando, FL: Harcourt, 1966), 34.

15. Ibid.

16. With thanks to Phil Schroeder for this translation.

17. Matthew 18:3; see also Matthew 19:14.

18. Isaiah 46:4, nasb.

19. Deuteronomy 33:27, rsv.

20. Mark 10:16.

CHAPTER 11: JESUS EITHER TALKED TOO MUCH OR WAS SILENT WHEN HE SHOULD HAVE TALKED

1. See Luke 9:12; 10:17, 38-42; John 1:12.

2. See Mark 2:1-12.

3. Mark 15:5.

4. Job 40:4.

5. Meister Eckhart, quoted in Trisha Day, *Inside the School of Charity* (Trappist, KY: Cistercian Publications, 2009).

6. See 1 Thessalonians 4:13.

7. See 1 Corinthians 13:12.

8. Author Robert J. Hutchinson writes, "In the past few decades, Jewish scholars have taken a closer look at the debates in the Gospels between Jesus and the Pharisees. For much of the twentieth century, skeptical New Testament scholars claimed that these debates were not historical—that

they reflected the conflicts the early church was having with Jewish authorities in the 80s and 90s and not what Jesus said and did in the 20s. But many Jewish experts now deny this. In addition, some Jewish scholars argue that the Gospels prove that Jesus had a thorough command of Jewish legal reasoning. According to Orthodox Rabbi Schmuley Boteach, when Jesus is criticized for healing a crippled man on the Sabbath (John 5:1-47), Jesus quotes a legal precedent preserved in the Talmud to prove that his action is justified. Boteach explains that the Torah commands that a male child be circumcised on the eighth day after birth, but if that day happens to fall on the Sabbath, the circumcision is still allowed even though it is 'drawing blood.' The Talmud draws from this exception the notion that medical procedures *can and must be done* on the Sabbath. According to Tractate Yoma, 'If circumcision, which concerns one of the 248 members of the body, overrides the Sabbath, shall not a man's whole body override the Sabbath?' Boteach then points to the *nearly identical reasoning* used by Jesus for his justification of healing a crippled man on the Sabbath, recorded by John: 'Now if a boy can be circumcised on the Sabbath so that the Law of Moses may not be broken,' Jesus says, 'why are you angry with me for healing a man's whole body on the Sabbath?' (7:23). This suggests that Jesus was not an 'illiterate peasant'— as many contemporary authors claim—but a *highly trained rabbi*, fully conversant with the complex legal and religious debates in his day." See Robert J. Hutchinson, "6 Shocking New Discoveries about Jesus of Nazareth," *The Blaze*, December 22, 2015, http://www.theblaze.com /contributions/6-shocking-new-discoveries-about-jesus-of-nazareth.

9. Jeremiah 17:13 says that those who turn away from the Lord will have their names written in the dust. Maybe Jesus wrote the names of those who were casting "first stones" in the dust.
10. Galatians 6:17.
11. See Jeremiah 31:33.
12. Matthew Battles, *Palimpsest: A History of the Written Word* (New York: W. W. Norton, 2015), 233.

CHAPTER 12: JESUS BROKE THE RULES
1. See Mark 2:27.
2. See Mark 2:28.
3. See Mark 3:4; cp. Matthew 12:12. See also Asher Intrater, *Who Ate Lunch with Abraham?* (Peoria, AZ: Intermedia, 2011), 47, 154–57.
4. Albert Nolan, *Jesus Today: A Spirituality of Radical Freedom* (Maryknoll, NY: Orbis, 2006), 55–56.

5. Ezekiel 36:26.
6. Matthew 15:10-11, 18, paraphrase.
7. See Luke 7:47.
8. Psalm 43:5.

CHAPTER 13: JESUS ENJOYED THE COMPANY OF WOMEN (NOT JUST MEN)

1. Matthew 12:7.
2. Matthew 5:7, paraphrase.
3. Nicholas King, "From the Beginning," *The Tablet*, December 12, 2015, 10.
4. See Matthew 19:1-12.
5. Matthew 5:28.
6. Proverbs 23:7, NKJV.
7. See Matthew 5:21-22.
8. See Mark 1:29-31; 5:41.
9. See Mark 5:21-43; Luke 7:11-17; 13:10-17; Matthew 15:21-28.
10. See Mark 12:43-44.
11. See Mark 14:9.
12. So said historian, geographer, and philosopher Strabo (ca. 64 BCE–ca. 24 CE).
13. Aristotle, *Generation of Animals*, trans. A. L. Peck (Cambridge, MA: Harvard University Press, 1942), 103, 133, 410–13, 406.
14. Thomas Aquinas, *Summa Theologica*, Question 92, Article 1. Reason on its own will always lead to weird places. See the reasoning in the "Burn the Witch!" segment of *Monty Python and the Holy Grail*, YouTube video, 5:32, posted by "A skeletin," October 20, 2007, http://www.youtube .com/watch?v=UTdDN_MRe64, accessed June 8, 2015.
15. See the chapter on women in *Thus Spake Zarathustra*, where Nietzsche also said "Everything about woman is a riddle."
16. Florence Nightingale, quoted in Frances Stonor Saunders, *The Woman Who Shot Mussolini* (New York: Henry Holt, 2010), 68.

CHAPTER 14: JESUS FOCUSED ON THE LITTLE THINGS IN LIFE

1. Matthew 18:20, RSV.
2. Zechariah 4:10.
3. Luke 17:6, NASB.
4. Matthew 19:26.
5. Zechariah 8:6.
6. Jesus' bad habit of choosing the worst to become the best drew the fire of the theologians and religious professionals of his day: "He is possessed by Beelzebul! By the prince of demons he is driving out demons" (Mark 3:22). *Beelzebul* means "lord of the flies" in Hebrew, "god of the dung

heaps" (where flies hang out) in Greek (*Beelzeboul*). Beelzebul was also one of the names the Jews gave to Satan.
7. So observed John Chrysostom.
8. See Matthew 16:3-7.
9. Gerald O'Collins, *Jesus: A Portrait* (Luton, UK: Andrews UK, 2008), 42.
10. Stephen Hawking, quoted in Kitty Ferguson, *Stephen Hawking: An Unfettered Mind* (New York: Macmillan, 2012), 70.
11. Psalm 8:3-5, NLT.

CHAPTER 15: JESUS THOUGHT HE WAS GOD
1. See John 8:56-58.
2. See John 1:1-3. John 17:5 is where Jesus declares that he shares the glory with his Father "before the world began."
3. Over twenty times you can find this. See Luke 10:16; John 4:34; 5:37-38.
4. See John 12:44-46; 14:6-9.
5. See Matthew 9:6-8; Luke 7:48-49; John 8:23-24.
6. See John 5:21-23; 6:40; 10:27-28; 11:25.
7. See the following references: John 10:30-33 (Jesus said he was the same as God); John 8:19; 14:7 (to know Jesus is to know God); John 12:44 (to hear Jesus is to hear God); John 12:45; 14:9 (to see Jesus is to see God); Mark 9:37 (to experience Jesus is to experience God); John 15:23 (to hate Jesus is to hate God); John 5:23 (to honor Jesus is to honor God).
8. Luke 2:49.
9. See Matthew 22:42-46.
10. See Luke 4:1-13 and 22:37-46.
11. Genesis 22:7-8.
12. There are only five references to Jesus' teachings in Paul's writings, only one of which quotes Jesus' words (1 Corinthians 11:23-26). For the other references see 1 Corinthians 7:10-11; 9:14; 14:37-38; 1 Thessalonians 4:15-17.
13. John 3:8.
14. Mark 10:18; Luke 18:19, NLT.
15. The Greek word *phanerósis* ("manifest") means to literally throb with a physical appearing.

CONCLUSION: BREAKING BAD
1. So also have said people like Duns Scotus (1264–1308) and so almost said John Calvin.
2. Also found in the *Christian Advocate*, January 20, 1921, 75.

Online Discussion *guide*

Take *your* Tyndale reading
experience *to the* next level

A FREE discussion guide for this book
is available at bookclubhub.net, perfect
for sparking conversations in your book
group or for digging deeper into the text
on your own.

www.bookclubhub.net

*You'll also find free discussion guides for
other Tyndale books, e-newsletters, e-mail
devotionals, virtual book tours, and more!*